NEUROCOMPUTATIONAL MODELS OF COGNITIVE DEVELOPMENT AND PROCESSING

PROGRESS IN NEURAL PROCESSING*

Series Advisor
Alan Murray *(University of Edinburgh)*

Vol. 11: Radial Basis Function Neural Networks with Sequential Learning
Eds. N. Sundararajan, P. Saratchandran & Y.-W. Lu

Vol. 12: Disorder Versus Order in Brain Function: Essays in Theoretical Neurobiology
Eds. P. Århem, C. Blomberg & H. Liljenström

Vol. 13: Business Applications of Neural Networks: The State-of-the-Art of Real-World Applications
Eds. Paulo J. G. Lisboa, Bill Edisbury & Alfredo Vellido

Vol. 14: Connectionist Models of Cognition and Perception
Eds. John A. Bullinaria & Will Lowe

Vol. 15: Connectionist Models of Cognition and Perception II
Eds. Howard Bowman & Christophe Labiouse

Vol. 16: Modeling Language, Cognition and Action
Eds. Angelo Cangelosi, Guido Bugmann & Roman Borisyuk

Vol. 17: From Associations to Rules: Connectionist Models of Behavior and Cognition
Eds. Robert M. French & Elizabeth Thomas

Vol. 18: Connectionist Models of Behaviour and Cognition II
Eds. Julien Mayor, Nicolas Ruh & Kim Plunkett

Vol. 19: Vision: Images, Signals and Neural Networks
By Jenny Hérault

Vol. 20: Connectionist Models of Neurocognition and Emergent Behavior
Ed. Eddy J. Davelaar

Vol. 21: Computational Models of Cognitive Processes
Eds. Julien Mayor & Pablo Gomez

Vol. 22: Neurocomputational Models of Cognitive Development and Processing: Proceedings of the 14th Neural Computation and Psychology Workshop
Eds. Katherine Twomey, Alastair Smith, Gert Westermann & Padraic Monaghan

*To view the complete list of the published volumes in the series, please visit:
http://www.worldscientific.com/series/pnp

Progress in Neural Processing • 22

Proceedings of the 14th Neural Computation and Psychology Workshop

NEUROCOMPUTATIONAL MODELS OF COGNITIVE DEVELOPMENT AND PROCESSING

Lancaster University, U.K. 21 – 23 August 2014

Editors

Katherine Twomey
Lancaster University, U.K.

Alastair Smith
Max Planck Institute for Psycholinguistics, The Netherlands

Gert Westermann
Lancaster University, U.K.

Padraic Monaghan
Lancaster University, U.K.

World Scientific

NEW JERSEY • LONDON • SINGAPORE • BEIJING • SHANGHAI • HONG KONG • TAIPEI • CHENNAI • TOKYO

Published by

World Scientific Publishing Co. Pte. Ltd.
5 Toh Tuck Link, Singapore 596224
USA office: 27 Warren Street, Suite 401-402, Hackensack, NJ 07601
UK office: 57 Shelton Street, Covent Garden, London WC2H 9HE

British Library Cataloguing-in-Publication Data
A catalogue record for this book is available from the British Library.

Progress in Neural Processing — Vol. 22
NEUROCOMPUTATIONAL MODELS OF COGNITIVE DEVELOPMENT AND PROCESSING
Proceedings of the 14th Neural Computation and Psychology Workshop

ISBN 978-981-4699-33-4

Printed in Singapore

Preface

The 14th Neural Computation and Psychology Workshop took place at Lancaster University (Lancaster, United Kingdom) from August 21st - 23rd, 2014. This volume is a collection of peer reviewed papers that together provide a sample of the research presented during the three-day conference. The theme of the workshop was 'Development across the lifespan' with submissions invited from researchers applying emergent models, largely but not exclusively of the connectionist/neural network kind, to investigate cognition.

The 14th meeting in the well-established Neural Computation and Psychology Workshop series continued the traditions of previous meetings bringing together researchers working across the fields of computer science, artificial intelligence, neurobiology, linguistics and psychology to discuss their work in an informal atmosphere designed to promote collaboration and communication between early career researchers and established investigators alike. The program maintained the single track structure with a limited number of high quality papers presented. The program also included keynote talks by Prof. James L. McClelland (Director, Center for Mind, Brain and Computation, Stanford University), Prof. Bob McMurray (Director, Mechanisms of Audio-Visual Categorization Lab, University of Iowa) and Prof. Michael Thomas (Director, Center for Educational Neuroscience, Birkbeck, University of London).

Mirroring the diversity of the workshop program this volume provides a collection of original contributions on a diverse yet complementary range of topics each on different aspects of cognition including: neural plasticity, hemispheric asymmetry, spoken and written word processing, visual object recognition and semantic knowledge representation.

As organisers of NCPW 14 we would like to thank all the attendees with special thanks to our keynote speakers. We would also like to thank EUCogIII (European Network for the Advancement of Artificial Cognitive Systems,

Interaction and Robotics) for their sponsorship of the event and this publication and the Faculty of Science, Lancaster University who also contributed financial support towards the hosting of NCPW 14. Further, Katherine E. Twomey, Gert Westermann and Padraic Monaghan are members of the International Centre for Language and Communicative Development (LuCiD) at Lancaster University. The support of the Economic and Social Research Council [ES/L008955/1] is thus gratefully acknowledged. We look forward to future instalments of the Neural Computation and Psychology Workshop.

Katherine Twomey, Alastair Smith, Gert Westermann and
Padraic Monaghan, NCPW 14 organisers.

Contents

Patchy Connectivity and Visual Processing Asymmetries: A Neurodevelopmental Hypothesis

Ben Cipollini

UC San Diego

Garrison W. Cottrell

UC San Diego

The existence of left-right asymmetries in classification of visual stimuli has been established by a long history of behavioral experiments and neuroimaging studies. The Double Filtering by Frequency (DFF) model [11] accounts for experimental data from four key publications, but offers no neural basis for a spatial frequency processing asymmetry it postulates to exist. The Differential Encoding (DE) model [10] is neurally inspired, but has accounted for very little experimental data and hasn't followed the underlying biology closely. In this paper, we address the issues with the DE model in three steps. First, we make a more direct mapping between the DE model and the connectivity asymmetry that inspired it. Second, we apply the model to a similar set of data accounted for by the DFF model. Third, we show that the proposed connectivity asymmetry can emerge through typical development, and corroborate the relationship between connectivity and spatial frequency processing. Overall, we find that this version of the DE model can account for three of the four datasets tested: processing of local/global levels in Navon figures [17] and using high/low frequency information based on task demands [13], and a dataset showing lateralization of face identification [21]. The final dataset is from an experiment used to demonstrate that it is relative frequency in the stimuli, not absolute frequency differences, that matter. We suggest that a deeper version of the model could account for the data in a neurally plausible way, using absolute frequency differences encountered at different stages of processing.

Keywords: Asymmetry; Differential Encoding; Double filtering by Frequency; Hierarchical Letter Stimuli; Lateralization; Visual Processing.

1. Introduction

A large literature of behavioral experiments and neuroimaging studies has established the existence of left-right asymmetries in classification tasks across a variety of visual stimuli. Typically, these studies have used visual half-field presentation, where a stimulus is briefly presented to the left or right of a fixation point, then subjects press a button to indicate their response to some type of classification task (such as whether a target stimulus was present or not). If the same stimulus is presented in the right visual field (RVF) and left visual field (LVF) and differences in reaction time or accuracy are found, then a hemispheric difference in the processing of the stimulus is inferred due to constrained connectivity in the brain, where information from the LVF is initially directed exclusively to the right cerebral hemisphere (RH), and information from the RVF to the left cerebral hemisphere (LH). Across these studies, the two inferences that are generally made are that the LH shows a specialization for processing information at higher spatial frequencies (HSF), while the RH shows a specialization for processing information at lower spatial frequencies (LSF)[7,11,17].

Ivry and Robertson[11] developed the Double Filtering by Frequency (DFF) theory to account for these visual half-field results as well as asymmetries in frequency processing of auditory stimuli. They proposed that, after early sensory encoding decomposes a stimulus into its component frequencies, processing involves two filtering stages. First, each hemisphere focuses on only the frequencies relevant to the task. Then, each hemisphere has a bias in encoding information within that band of task-relevant frequencies: the LH encodes more information in the higher frequencies of those selected in the first stage, while the RH encodes more spectral power in the lower frequencies of those selected.

To provide some validation of their theory, Ivry and Robertson also implemented a neural network model based on the DFF theory. This model was able to account for three particular experiments from the literature, each of which Ivry and Robertson argued expresses a core feature of visual processing asymmetries. These include a study of local/global processing, and two studies examining classification of spatial frequency gratings. Later, Hsiao *et al.*[9] implemented a different neural network model of the DFF theory, and showed that it could account for a fourth study on face processing (see Table 1 for more information on these studies).

While the DFF theory and associated models account for all of these data, Hsiao *et al.*[10] questioned some of the assumptions and implementation details of these models, including:

- There is a lack of physiological evidence suggesting differential frequency tuning in the neurons of the two hemispheres.
- The stimuli were drastically reduced in complexity relative to the experimental stimuli: they used 1D arrays (instead of 2D images) with only 2 stimulus classes (instead of the 6 presented to human subjects).
- The classification task used to train their model differed from that given to human subjects.
- With further training, their hemisphere $\times$ level interaction disappeared or reversed.

To address this, Hsiao *et al.*[10] developed a neural network model with a simple architectural difference between the hemispheres. Specifically, they incorporated an anatomical asymmetry in long-range lateral connections between "patches" found in Wernicke's area (a language-related auditory area) and its RH homologue[4] into a simple autoencoder neural network. These connections selectively interconnect a subset of nearby patches, or macro columns, and are involved in combining information across classic receptive fields. This Differential Encoding (DE) model was used to encode 2D images of Navon figures (large "global"-level letters composed of smaller "local"-level letters); when these encodings were then classified with a second neural network, the same hemisphere $\times$ level interaction emerged.

While suggestive, this model was used to account for only one of the four experiments that the DFF has accounted for. In addition, the DE model did not use biologically plausible parameters, nor was the specific role of the connections in question justified in the experiment modeled. Finally, how or why this connectivity difference might occur during development was never addressed.

We aim to address all of these issues here. We begin by arguing that long-range lateral connections are likely to be involved in the experimental paradigms found to elicit visual processing asymmetries, due to their activation when stimulus strength is low. We argue that the DE model, with a specific configuration, is a reasonable implementation of the anatomical system. We then describe modeling experiments where we implemented this model setup, and showed that such a model exhibits both spatial frequency differences, as well as differences on classification tasks of encoded stimuli, for three of the behavioral studies that the DFF has accounted for. We discuss why we think a failure to account for the fourth study is informative and potentially interesting. Finally, to support the plausibility of our work, we show, using a developmental version of our model, that normal neural development of visual cortex, in conjunction with changes in visual acuity and a hypothesized timing difference in the maturation of the hemispheres, can lead to the hypothesized anatomical asymmetry.

2. Patchy connectivity may be involved in processing asymmetries

Patches are groups of locally interconnected mini-columns, spanning about 500um in diameter in cortex. They are called patches because an injection of dye into the cortical surface will label cortex at the injection site, as well as a number of discrete patches of surrounding cortex. They are thought to be functional units, and somewhat akin to hypercolumns. These patches themselves interconnect with nearby patches within a cortical area through long-range lateral connections that travel through the grey matter. These patchy connection networks are quite specific and sparse; a patch will connect with a subset of its local neighbors [14].

Why might long-range lateral connections be specifically involved in Sergent's experiment, or other experiments showing visual processing asymmetries and accounted for by Ivry and Robertson's DFF model? Looking into the literature, we found a number of reviews showing that asymmetries were quite dependent on task setup and stimulus parameters, specifically stimulus contrast and stimulus presentation duration: stimuli must be presented with low contrast, or briefly, to elicit asymmetries [2,11,18,19]. When the stimulus strength is high, asymmetries disappear.

We interpret these findings to suggest that asymmetry is not in the feed-forward pathway, whose function we assume is positively correlated to stimulus strength, but instead can be found in secondary types of connections - feed-back and long-range lateral connections. We focus on long-range lateral connections between patches because they have specifically been found to be more active during low stimulus strength [20], are well characterized anatomically and physiologically [14], are thought to help encode higher-level visual information such as contours [5,6], and as described above, we know of at least one existing asymmetry in this type of connectivity [4].

We find that a specific implementation of the neural network employed by Hsiao *et al.* to be a plausible model of how long-range lateral connections affect a map-based encoding, such as a retinotopic encoding of an image. Specifically, connections from the input to hidden layer can be interpreted as a recurrent network unfolded in time, if each hidden unit connects to the input image at that hidden unit's location. In this particular model architecture, forward propagation of activity along the input-to-hidden unit connections would represent the propagation of activity laterally, over one time-step. The number of hidden units used would represent the number of local patchy connection networks used to reconstruct the image; when the number of hidden units matches the number of pixels, then all patchy connection networks are used in the reconstruction.

2.1. *Methods*

The Differential Encoding (DE) model consists of two autoencoder neural networks, each representing one cerebral hemisphere, which differ only in the spatial spread of connections from the input to hidden, and hidden to output layers. Unlike most autoencoders, the hidden units of these models connect to a small subset of the input and output banks (see Figure 1). Each hidden unit has a position in the input (and output) arrays, and a fixed number of connections to the input (and

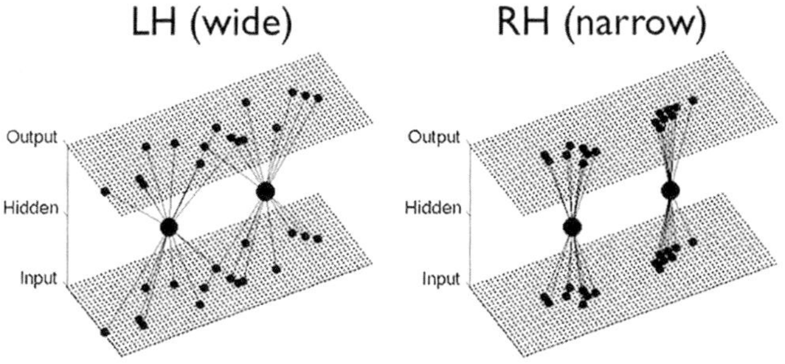

Fig. 1. Representation of two hidden units for LH (left) and RH (right) autoencoder networks, along with their connections. The connections are randomly sampled from a Gaussian distribution centered on each hidden unit's position in the input array. The Gaussian distribution used for the LH is wider than that used for the RH. Not pictured are the classification networks, which operate on the hidden unit encodings extracted from the autoencoder networks after training.

output) arrays are sampled from a Gaussian distribution centered at that hidden unit's position in the input (and output). The LH and RH autoencoders have the same number of hidden units and sample the same number of connections to the input (and output) for each hidden unit. The only difference between the networks, then, is the width (σ) of the Gaussian distribution.

In accordance with the findings of Galuske *et al.*[4], the LH network has a wider distribution than the RH network (see Figure 1). Note that this differs from previous models of hemispheric differences, where the Gaussian describes the receptive fields of Radial Basis Function units[15]. In that work, wider receptive fields characterize the RH. Here, *whether or not there is a connection* is sampled from a Gaussian distribution. Our connections are sparse and there is no center-surround receptive field structure. Based on previous results in Hsiao *et al.*, we expected to find the opposite associations in this network architecture: a wider connection distribution would favor processing of HSFs, and a more narrow connection distribution would favor processing of LSFs.

The number of hidden units was set to the number of pixels (34×25 pixels $= 850$), to allow equal spacing across the input image with enough total parameters to learn the images. The number of connections per hidden unit (15) were fixed to be close to values reported in the literature for the number of interconnecting patches labeled by a single injection in V4[1][a]. Each LH and RH network

[a]A wide range of values (smaller and larger) was tested for each of these parameters; results did not differ qualitatively when the number of connections per hidden unit varied to allow for the same number of overall weights to be used to learn the images. If too few weights were used, the networks could not learn the training set well enough for a meaningful analysis.

was constructed by randomly sampling connections for each hidden node. Gaussian distributions were used such that inter-patch distance values were similar to those reported in Galuske *et al.*, computed as the relative width of a "patch" (here, considered to be 1 pixel) vs. the relative distance between the center of patches (1.75 for the RH, 2.05 for the LH).

Table 1. The following four behavioral studies are addressed in the current modeling experiments.

Reference	Description
Sergent (1982)	Using Navon figures (large "global"-level letters composed of smaller "local"-level letters), this study showed a hemisphere × level interaction, where target letters present at the larger, global level generally elicited a faster reaction times when presented to the LVF/RH, while target letters present at the smaller, local level generally elicited faster reaction times when presented to the RVF/LH.
Kitterle *et al.* (1992)	This study showed that the same stimuli used in different tasks could elicit different hemispheric advantages. This suggests that it is not the frequencies present in the stimuli alone that elicit the asymmetry in processing, but rather which frequencies are relevant to the task that drive the asymmetry. They found that a task requiring HSF information (square vs. sine waves, ignoring the frequency of the waves) elicited faster reaction times when stimuli were presented to the RVF/LH, while a task requiring LSF information (distinguishing two low frequency gratings, ignoring whether they are square or sine waves) elicited faster reaction times when stimuli were presented to the LVF/RH.
Christman *et al.* (1991)	This study showed that when two stimuli differed by a single spatial frequency, which hemisphere showed a processing advantage didn't depend on the actual frequency of that component, but rather whether that frequency was relatively higher or lower compared to the other frequencies composing the stimuli. When the discriminative frequency was higher than the frequency content of the rest of the stimulus, responses were faster for presentation to the RVF/LH; when the discriminative frequency was lower than the frequency content of the rest of the stimulus, responses were faster for presentation to the LVF/RH.
Young & Bion (1981)	This study showed that accuracy on a face identification task was better when the probe faces were presented to the LVF/RH. It has been shown elsewhere that the RH may be dominant for face identification due to its advantage for low frequency processing[9], so we choose to test our model on this task as well.

We aimed to model the four datasets described in Table 1. Each of these four datasets were collected using brief, lateralized presentation of an image, then requiring some classification of that stimulus (e.g. whether the stimulus contained a target feature or not). We assume that asymmetries elicited in this paradigm are due to hemispheric differences in encoding these stimuli, and asymmetries in the classification of these stimuli are due to the asymmetries of the encodings. Our basic model setup, then, is to construct greyscale images for each task; to encode these images in our LH and RH autoencoder models with asymmetric connectivity patterns, and then to classify these asymmetric encodings in separate, but identical, LH and RH feed-forward neural networks trained on the classification task corresponding to the encoded images for that dataset.

For each dataset, greyscale images were constructed for each task stimulus. The autoencoders were trained via backpropagation of error[16], using batch processing and the sum-squared error (SSE) cost function, to reproduce these greyscale images from the input to the output. Once the autoencoders reached a pre-determined performance level ($SSE = 0.02$, per output unit), training stopped. We used two types of regularization (weight decay (each iteration, every weight is multiplied by $\lambda = 0.975$) and adding noise (0.01%) to our training images) to encourage good generalization. Each stimulus image was presented to the trained autoencoder network, and the activation of the hidden units was recorded. These encodings, which differed only due to the differences in connectivity structure between LH and RH networks, were then used as inputs to a separate 3-layer feed-forward neural network, which was trained to classify these encoded stimuli according to the behavioral task given to human subjects in the original experiment. The number of hidden units was different for each classification network (but identical between hemispheres), and was chosen such that the classification task could be learned well. We chose to separate general visual encoding (our autoencoder network) from task performance (our perceptron), to reflect the idea that retinotopic visual encoding is established during early visual experience and does not change during task performance. In subsequent work, we train our autoencoder networks with natural images to further substantiate this idea.

For a single experiment, multiple instances of each LH and RH network were constructed and trained; each instance differs only in the random sampling of its connections.[b] Performance was evaluated on each model individually, then performance for all instances of each hemisphere were averaged. Average model error for each model hemisphere was compared to average reaction time in the corresponding human experiment, with both conceived as measures of difficulty or uncertainty in processing.

[b]The number of model instances was chosen such that the total number of trials across all stimuli and model instances matched that reported in the corresponding behavioral experiment, to match statistical power of results.

In order to examine how the different connectivity distributions affect spatial frequency encoding, each stimulus image was presented to a trained autoencoder. Each output image produced was examined for spatial frequency content, and a 2D spectrogram across all images in the stimulus set was constructed. Each 2D spectrogram was translated to a 1D spectrogram.[c] Each spectrogram was compared to the spectrogram of the original image; the absolute value of the difference between the spectrograms represents the error for each model hemisphere's encoding at each spatial frequency. This error measure was then compared across hemispheres, showing for each frequency which hemisphere has encoded information closer to the original image than the other.

2.2. *Results*

Results are summarized in Table 2, showing that for three of the four tasks, the model performance (column 2) showed the interaction or performance differences found in the human behavioral measures (column 1). In addition, in all four tasks, the model shows an interaction between frequency band and hemisphere (column 3): greater accuracy in reproducing images for the RH networks (above zero-line) is focused in the lower spatial frequencies (towards origin), while greater accuracy for the LH networks (below zero-line) is focused in the higher spatial frequencies (away from origin).

This indicates that, somewhat counterintuitively, narrowly distributed connections are biased relatively more towards LSF processing, and widely distributed connections are biased relatively more towards HSF processing. We are investigating the cause of this relationship in current work. Preliminary results indicate that average spacing between nearest-neighbors of input/output units connecting to a single hidden unit governs this behavior. Specifically, when connection spread is small, constructive/destructive interference patterns between LSF vs HSF gratings of different phases and orientations occur: LSF gratings shows large variations in hidden unit activation based on particular orientations and phases, while HSF gratings do not. This seems to allow for more specific encoding of shapes and contours in LSF gratings, and thus a bias towards representing LSF information.

Examining these results more closely, we found two places where our models did not accurately reflect the human behavior. In our replication of Kitterle *et al.*, while we did show the measured hemisphere $\times$ task interaction, the relative difficulty of the two tasks did not match that in the human measures. This diffi-

---

[c]Each 2D frequency (f_x, f_y) was converted to a 1D frequency $(f_r = \sqrt{f_x^2 + f_y^2})$; for each unique value of f_r, all power/amplitude values were then averaged to create the 1D spectrogram.

Table 2. Simulation results, comparing human & simulation output

	Human Data	Simulation Data	Spatial Frequency Processing
Sergent (1982)	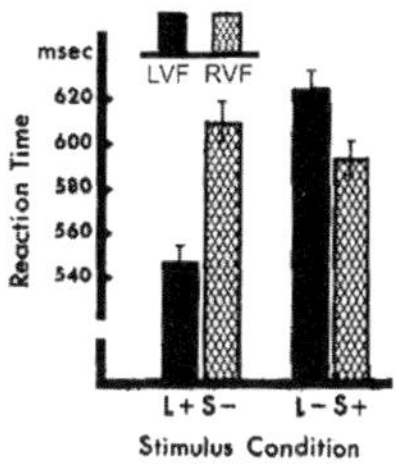	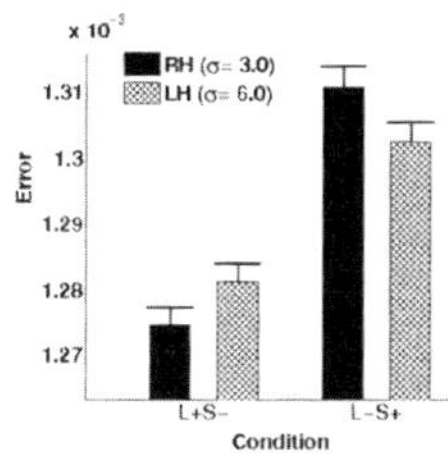	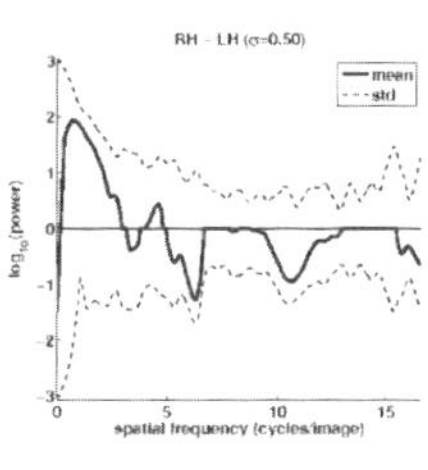
Kitterle et al. (1992)	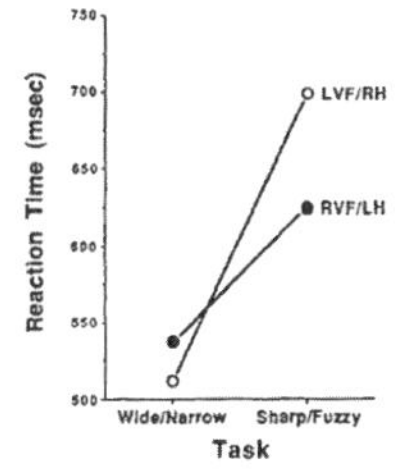	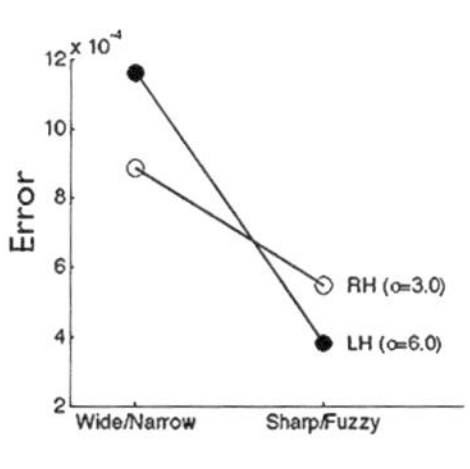	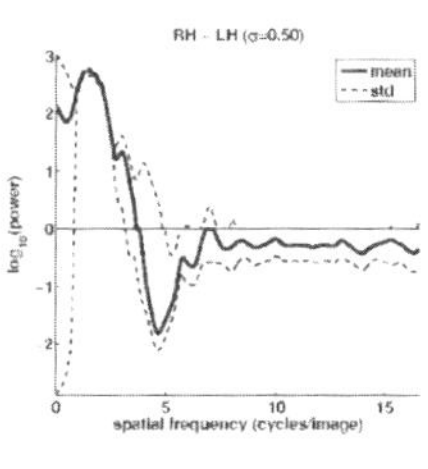
Young & Bion (1981)	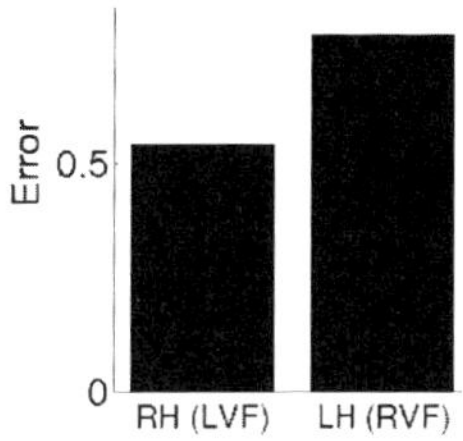	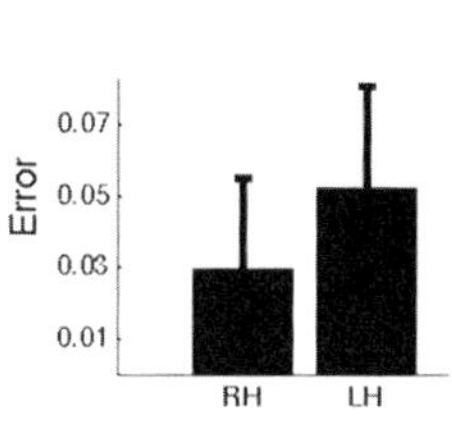	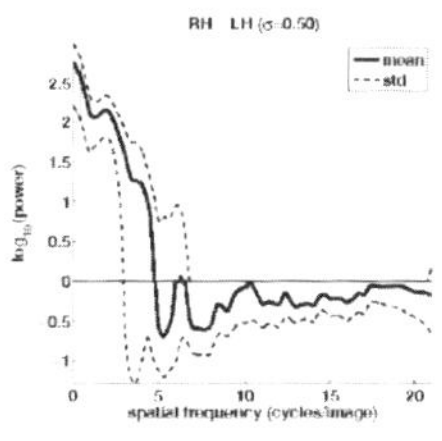
Christman et al. (1991)	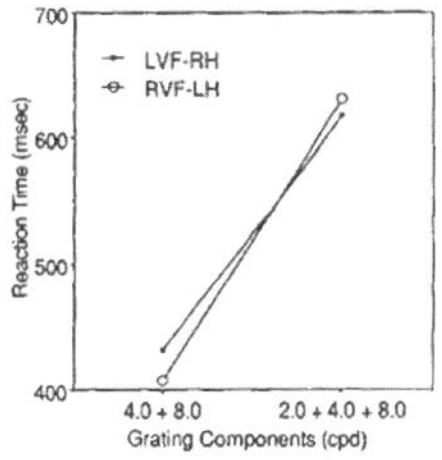	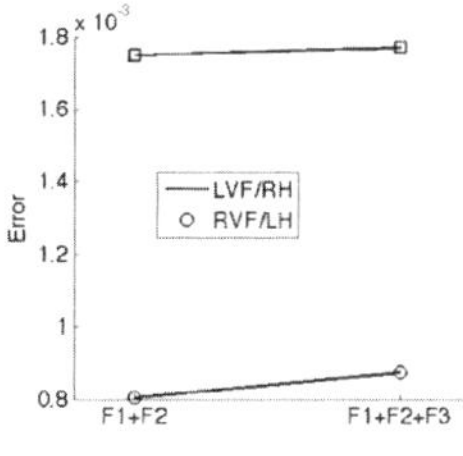	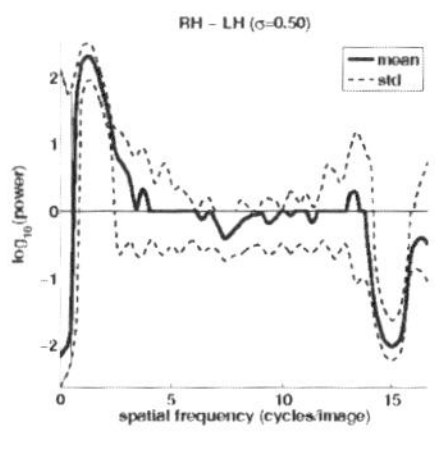

culty may depend on different sensory transformations, or other issues. In fact, in subsequent work, we have found this to be true in the modeling; changing the training dataset, or regularization parameters, does not affect the hemisphere × task interaction, but does affect the relative difficulty of the two tasks. Therefore, we don't think that this mismatch is a critical issue to consider further here.

We believe the second issue we found is more important, and more interesting. Our models did *not* show a hemisphere × stimulus class interaction for the Christman *et al.* study. We tested a few possible explanations for this. We varied the three base frequencies that composed the stimuli; this affected which model hemisphere showed better performance, but no reliable hemisphere × stimulus class interaction was found. We tried larger images, to expand the range of spatial frequencies that could be encoded and obtained similar results. Lastly, we trained the autoencoder on a separate dataset, then extracting hidden unit encodings on the task-relevant stimuli. Again, this did not show any consistent interaction.

Using data from our developmental model, we discuss an alternative interpretation of the Christman *et al.* study in the Discussion section below.

3. Patchy connection networks may develop asymmetrically in humans, under normal visual development

The results above clearly suggest an association between narrowly distributed connections and LSF processing, and widely distributed connections and HSF processing. Here, we investigated whether a developmentally-inspired model can learn these connection patterns through experience. The model incorporates three observations/constraints: 1) The right hemisphere begins maturing earlier than the left; 2) early in development, the input to the system is concentrated in the low spatial frequencies, due to low acuity in infancy; and 3) synaptic connections are subject to a pruning process to remove weak or ineffective connections.

This setup has strong parallels with human visual development. Hellige[7] has provided evidence that the RH begins maturing earlier than the LH. We know that visual acuity changes rapidly in infants, such that visual acuity and sensitivity to high frequencies increases over time. This means that the RH will mature while visual input is more biased towards low frequencies, and the LH will mature while the visual input is less biased. Katz and Callaway[12] have shown that connections between patches mature by strengthening connections consistent with visual input, and pruning (removing) connections that are not. Thus, our goal is not only to try and corroborate our previous findings, but to provide a plausible neurodevelopmental account of where both anatomical and behavioral asymmetries come from.

3.1. *Methods*

We created two sets of autoencoder neural networks, each completely identical. They each had the same connectivity pattern, consisting of 20 connections selected from a circular 2D Gaussian distribution from the hidden units to the input and output units, with a fixed number of connections from each hidden unit to the input and output layers. The only difference between these sets of neural networks was that one was trained on blurred, low-frequency-passed images (our RH networks) and the other was trained on full-fidelity images (our LH networks), to simulate differences in development. As a first pass, we used a Gaussian kernel (σ=8px) to blur our images for the RH network.

Networks were trained using back propagation of error (batch mode, using SSE as described above), to simulate the strengthening of connections through learning. To simulate the pruning aspect of development, after every 10 epochs, we removed a constant percentage of the weakest connections (13.4%), such that after 50 epochs exactly 50% of the connections remained. At the end of training, each network had a 50% reduction in its original connections, such that on average, each hidden unit had 10 connections.

3.2. *Results*

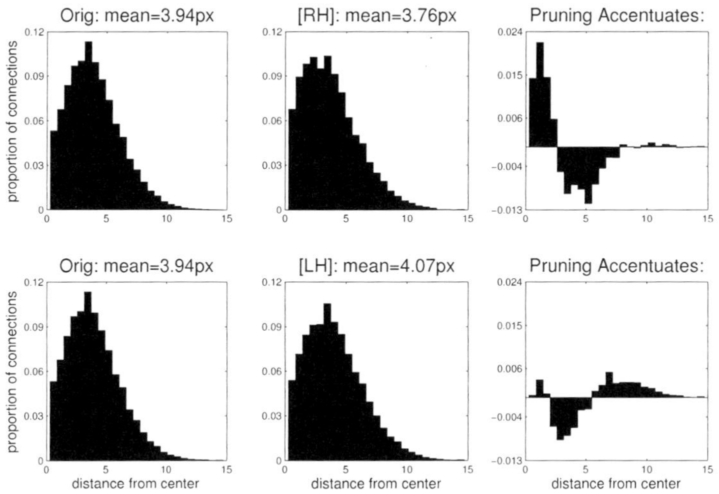

Fig. 2. Distribution of connections for networks trained on blurry/low-pass (RH; top row) and full-fidelity (LH; bottom row) images, as well as the difference between each of those distributions from the original distribution.

After training, the network trained on low-pass/blurry images (RH) biased the original distribution towards shorter connections, while the network trained on full-fidelity images (LH) biased the original distribution towards more distant connections (see Fig. 2). This corroborated the associations we saw in our first study, where a smaller spread of connections favored storing information in LSFs, and where a wider spread of connections favored storing information in HSFs. Analysis of the spectral power differences between the networks also showed a similar bias as described in Table 2.

We are examining the computational reasons behind this association in current work.

4. Reprising the "relative frequency" effect

Christman *et al.*[3] showed that when a frequency grating alone distinguished two stimulus classes, the effect of that grating depended on the frequency of that grating *relative* to the other frequencies that made up those stimuli. When the distinguishing grating was higher than the rest of the frequencies used in the stimuli, the stimulus containing the distinguishing grating showed a LH advantage; when the distinguishing grating was lower, there was a RH advantage. Ivry and Robertson propose that this "relative frequency" effect is itself a computational mechanism: filters at different spatial scales / frequency bands are weighted and summed based on the task; a top-down bias to those weights (that differs between the hemispheres) is relative to the the frequencies selected by those weights.

An alternate hypothesis is that the same filters that select the task-based frequency range are themselves different between the hemispheres. Then, when those filters are weighted and summed based on task demands, a bias that is dependent on that weighting occurs. This alternate hypothesis is not possible in the DFF, where the filters represent bottom-up processing in all conditions (low and high stimulus strength), and therefore would predict hemispheric differences in every experiment. This alternate hypothesis is possible with our model, however. We argued that long-range lateral connections are only active during low stimulus strength, as found in the experiments detailed above. In our case, different "filters" would be different cortical areas, each of which process information at different spatial scales.

Looking to the literature, and examining unpublished simulations, we find data consistent with our proposal. Tasks at different spatial scales do engage different cortical areas[8], consistent with our suggestion that cortical areas can act as task-based filters of spatial scale / frequency. Using this idea in our developmental model suggests that homologous cortical areas between LH and RH would have different frequency biases *relative to the spatial scale of that area.* In that model, we found that small reductions (due to synaptic pruning) in the average spread of long-range lateral connections biases processing towards LSFs. Further experiments with our developmental model showed that, the greater the original spread of connections, the lower the frequency at which the RH stopped showing an advantage (the cross-over point, where RH and LH performance is similar). Thus, in our proposal, homologous areas with larger spatial scales would have to have a larger average spread of connections in order show a frequency bias relative to that spatial scale. In fact, that's exactly what's found in the macaque monkey: areas higher in the visual processing hierarchy show longer average connections, both in cortical distance, and in the percentage of the visual field they span over [1]. Our modeling data also suggest that, given the small average spread found in early visual areas, little or no frequency biases could develop there. This is consistent with the idea that visual processing asymmetries are found beyond early sensory processing.

Thus, the failure of our model to account for Christman *et al.*'s data may indicate that these data represent processing in two different cortical areas, each selective for information at a particular spatial scale, each with frequency processing biases relative to that spatial scale. Our autoencoder model above represents a single cortical area; to model this, we would need multiple autoencoder models, each with information at different spatial scales (possibly different image resolutions) and with corresponding changes to the average connections spread (greater for images of lower resolutions).

5. Discussion

Here we showed that an asymmetry in a specific type of intra-cortical connectivity can account for local/global behavioral data, face processing data, and matches spatial frequency asymmetries reported in the literature. This model provides a biologically grounded implementation for these phenomena, and the analyses here showing consistent frequency filtering differences in the model hemispheres are consistent with the current algorithmic explanation for visual processing asymmetries via frequency filtering. These frequency filtering differences are found at a post-sensory encoding stage, consistent with the suggestions in the literature.

We have also implemented a plausible developmental scenario for the emergence of this connectivity asymmetry, which uses three principles supported by developmental data (changes in visual acuity over development, both strengthening and pruning of long-range lateral connections during development, and different time-courses for RH and LH maturation).

Finally, we have suggested that our failure to model the results of Christman *et al.* with a model of a single cortical area is not a failure of our model, but instead suggests that the "relative frequency" effect in visual processing asymmetries is itself not a mechanism in visual processing. We propose that this effect is the result of latent biases within higher areas in the visual hierarchy that are established developmentally and are relative to that area's spatial scale of processing. The bias of an area affects visual processing when the spatial scale of processing for a task matches that of the area, and when stimulus strength is sufficiently weak to activate these intrinsic long-range lateral connections.

Acknowledgments

This research was funded in part by a CARTA (Center for Research and Training in Anthropogeny) Fellowship, and by NSF grant SMA 1041755 to the Temporal Dynamics of Learning Center.

References

1. Amir, Y., Harel, M. and Malach, R. (1993). Cortical hierarchy reflected in the organization of intrinsic connections in macaque monkey visual cortex, *The Journal of Comparative Neurology* **334**, 1, pp. 19–46.
2. Christman, S. (1989). Perceptual characteristics in visual laterality research, *Brain and Cognition* **11**, 2, pp. 238–257.
3. Christman, S., Kitterle, F. L. and Hellige, J. (1991). Hemispheric asymmetry in the processing of absolute versus relative spatial frequency, *Brain and Cognition* **16**, 1, pp. 62–73.
4. Galuske, R. A., Schlote, W., Bratzke, H. and Singer, W. (2000). Interhemispheric asymmetries of the modular structure in human temporal cortex, *Science (New York, N.Y.)* **289**, 5486, pp. 1946–1949.
5. Gilbert, C. D. (1992). Horizontal integration and cortical dynamics, *Neuron* **9**, 1, pp. 1–13.
6. Grossberg, S. and Williamson, J. R. (2001). A neural model of how horizontal and interlaminar connections of visual cortex develop into adult circuits that carry out perceptual grouping and learning, *Cerebral Cortex* **11**, 1, pp. 37–58.
7. Hellige, J. B. (1993). *Hemispheric Asymmetry: What's Right and What's Left* (Harvard University Press), ISBN 0674005597.
8. Hopf, J., Luck, S. J., Boelmans, K., Schoenfeld, M. A., Boehler, C. N., Rieger, J. and Heinze, H. (2006). The neural site of attention matches the spatial scale of perception, *The Journal of Neuroscience* **26**, 13, pp. 3532–3540.

9. Hsiao, J., Shahbazi, R. and Cottrell, G. (2008). Hemispheric asymmetry in visual perception arises from differential encoding beyond the sensory level, *Proceedings of the 30th Annual Meeting of the Cognitive Science Society*.
10. Hsiao, J. H.-w., Shieh, D. X. and Cottrell, G. W. (2008). Convergence of the visual field split: Hemispheric modeling of face and object recognition, *Journal of Cognitive Neuroscience* **20**, 12, pp. 2298–2307.
11. Ivry, R. B. and Robertson, L. C. (1998). *The Two Sides of Perception* (The MIT Press), ISBN 0262090341.
12. Katz, L. C. and Callaway, E. M. (1992). Development of local circuits in mammalian visual cortex, *Annual Review of Neuroscience* **15**, 1, pp. 31–56.
13. Kitterle, F. L., Hellige, J. B. and Christman, S. (1992). Visual hemispheric asymmetries depend on which spatial frequencies are task relevant, *Brain and Cognition* **20**, 2, pp. 308–314.
14. Levitt, J. and Lund, J. (2002). Intrinsic connections in mammalian cerebral cortex, in A. Schuez and R. Miller (eds.), *Cortical areas: unity and diversity* (CRC Press), ISBN 9780415277235, pp. 133–154.
15. Monaghan, P. and Shillcock, R. (2004). Hemispheric asymmetries in cognitive modeling: Connectionist modeling of unilateral visual neglect, *Psychological Review* **111**, 2, pp. 283–308.
16. Rumelhart, D. E., Hinton, G. E. and Williams, R. J. (1986). Learning representations by back-propagating errors, *Nature* **323**, 6088, pp. 533–536.
17. Sergent, J. (1982). The cerebral balance of power: confrontation or cooperation? *Journal of Experimental Psychology. Human Perception and Performance* **8**, 2, pp. 253–72.
18. Sergent, J. (1983). Role of the input in visual hemispheric asymmetries, *Psychological Bulletin* **93**, 3, pp. 481–512.
19. Sergent, J. (1985). Influence of task and input factors on hemispheric involvement in face processing, *Journal of Experimental Psychology. Human Perception and Performance* **11**, 6, pp. 846–861.
20. Swadlow, H. A. and Alonso, J. (2009). Spikes are making waves in the visual cortex, *Nat Neurosci* **12**, 1, pp. 10–11.
21. Young, A. W. and Bion, P. J. (1981). Accuracy of naming laterally presented known faces by children and adults, *Cortex; a Journal Devoted to the Study of the Nervous System and Behavior* **17**, 1, pp. 97–106.

Neural Binding in Letter- and Word-Recognition

P. H. de Vries
Department of Experimental Psychology, University of Groningen
The Netherlands
E-mail: p.h.de.vries@rug.nl
www.rug.nl/staff/p.h.de.vries

The reading of a word can be used to illustrate the cognitive phenomena of the formation and decomposition of a chunk: a skilled reader perceives a word as a whole and can also report the letter at a certain position in a word. These processes pose a challenge to models of the brain that are based on biologically plausible principles of self-organisation. In most current models of word reading, it is not possible to go down from the word to the letter level for a specific letter position, or this process does not meet the requirements of self-organisation. A general model for the self-organisation of information-processing in the brain will be described: a conceptual network. In the application of this general model to the domain of letter- and word-recognition, the role of position in the perception of a word and in the identification of its letters becomes clear. Temporary connections (neural binding) play a fundamental role in the model as re-entrant pathways that come into existence during the perception of a word, and that are reactivated when a certain letter has to be identified. In simulations of the model the essential role of a critical threshold for the activation level of cell-assemblies has been shown, and the selective propagation of excitation loops at different time scales, during perception and response. Relations with recent empirical work on visual word-recognition and follow-up studies on self-organisation will be discussed.

Keywords: Binding; Cell-assemblies; Self-organisation; Letter- and word-recognition.

1. Introduction

The model presented in this paper is based on principles of self-organisation. These imply that that all behaviour and development of a system is explained as being the product of local interactions of elements distinguished in the system. One of the main problems in biologically plausible, self-organising models of cognition is the binding problem: how do two independent representations become combined without an agent that takes care of it? Accordingly, binding is seen as a process in the brain and it will be referred to as neural binding. In most existing models of word-processing[1], neural binding does not play a prominent role. Nonetheless its necessity follows imperatively from the theoretical argument that the internal representations of the identity and location of an object must be separate. If this is not the case, an unrealistically large number of memory traces would be needed, also referred to as a superposition catastrophe[2]. However, the argument continues: if identity and location are represented separately then binding is necessary. Otherwise essential distinctions between letter combinations in word-processing could not be made, for example the difference between letter combinations ‘ab’ and ‘ba’. In the present paper we will introduce binding as an essential part of a model of letter and word-processing.

The domain of letter and word-processing is an area of long-standing research in psychology and it has some well-established findings, such as the word-superiority effect and effects of masked priming[1]. The former refers to the phenomenon that a letter is recognized better when it is part of a word than when it is presented in isolation or as part of a non-word. In an experiment that makes use of masked priming a target stimulus, either a word or non-word, is preceded by a mask followed by a briefly presented a sequence of letters, the prime. Because of the mask and the short presentation time, the prime is not perceived consciously. Nonetheless the prime facilitates the recognition of a word target, if the letters in the prime are in the same relative order as in the target. The facilitation of non-word targets is less strong, if present at all.

Most existing models of word-processing are described at a functional level. This means that they are information-processing models and that they do not describe mechanisms necessary for biologically plausible self-organisation. If we want to study these mechanisms, we have to choose a lower level of description. This level will be referred to as the structural level. Some models of letter- and word-recognition do contain parts that refer to this level. In this context, a historic example is the interactive-activation model[3,4], that provided important new ways of thinking about the word-superiority effect and cognitive processes in general. Many other models have followed, especially in relation to experiments on masked priming. A comparison of these models and their levels of description would exceed the available space but is given in [5].

The paper will comprise a general cognitive model based on self-organisation, its application to letter- and word-processing, its simulation, and proposals for new experiments. Next to binding, the principles of self-organisation of the model, can also be used to explain learning and development. In particular, the paper will show that the choice for a model based on self-organisation constrains the results of learning and development,. as all changes in a system have to work with that which is already there. Moreover, these changes have to take place while the system is functioning. It cannot be put in a dock to be modified. Accordingly, the choice for a model based on self-organisation constrains the nature and number of modules in a system. In a functional model of letter- and word-processing, for example, modules can be distinguished that are not plausible from a point of view of self-organisation, as we shall see later in this paper.

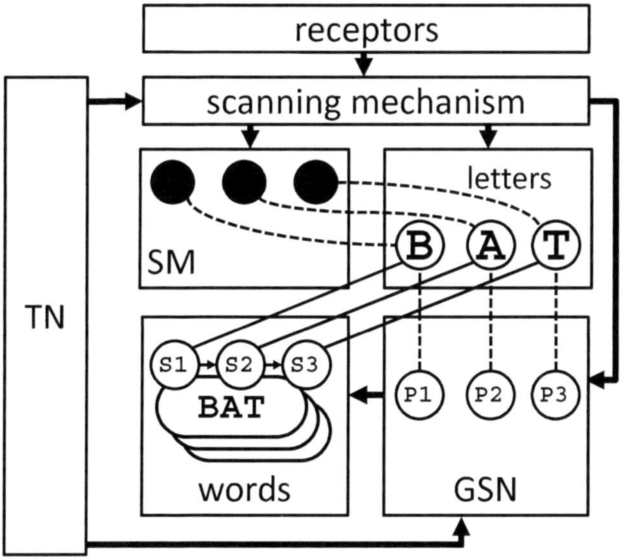

Fig. 1. Conceptual network for letter- and word-recognition, rectangles indicate modules for the input (receptors, scanning mechanism), a spatial map (SM), subnetworks for letters and words, a global sequence network (GSN) and a task network (TN), the arrows and solid lines indicate the activation of one module by another by means of permanent connections, a dashed line represents a temporary connection (binding).

The word-superiority effect shows that we perceive a word as a single chunk. The reverse process, the decomposition of chunk into its elements poses a challenge to models of cognitive self-organisation. It pertains to the question 'what is the *n*-th letter of a given word?' For adult readers and short words, the answer to this question can be easily given. At a structural level of description, the generation of this answer implies that a position-specific top-down activation from the word to the letter level must exist. Apart from the model described in this paper, the author does not know of any other model of self-organisation that provides an adequate account for this top-down process.

In relation to the principles of self-organisation, the following two restrictions will be applied:

1. The network proposed in this paper is not (yet) the result of a process of autonomous development. It is a designed network. At the present state of research, we still lack the insights necessary for the self-organising development of systems that are biologically plausible and that can perform tasks at a cognitively realistic level. However, the design of a network based on biologically plausible mechanisms *is* possible. This approach provides insights into the end product of an autonomous developmental process. These insights are essential to find the conditions necessary for cognitive self-organisation to take place.
2. In this paper the focus will be on the logistics of the self-organisation of excitation processes. We will refrain from a detailed discussion of neuroanatomical and neurophysiological issues. The presented model is based on biologically plausible properties of neurons and it is general enough to accommodate more neuro-scientific properties at a later stage.

The architecture of the network for letter- and word-recognition, discussed in this paper is shown Figure 1. It will be referred to as a conceptual network since its nodes represent memory traces, which in the context of this paper are considered to be concepts. A conceptual network is a general cognitive model. Next to letter- and word-recognition, it can be applied to other cognitive domains[6-7].

2. Self-Organisation

In order to construct a conceptual network on the basis of self-organisation, three forms of local interaction play an essential role[6,7]. All three of them qualify as a form of coincidence of activation.

Coincidence of activation in a pair of neurons. Although learning will not be part of the simulations shown in the paper, it does play a role in a number of theoretical arguments for the model. We will first consider the learning rule of Hebb[8] and others before him, notably Tanzi[9], which states that simultaneous activity of a pair of neurons leads to a more efficient synaptic connection between them. Hebb already argued that the formation of cell-assemblies is a consequence of the rule. He defined a cell-assembly as a cluster of neurons having more and stronger connections with each other than with neurons in other clusters. At the functional level, each cell-assembly corresponds to a memory trace or concept. Already in the 1940's it had to be assumed that the neurons of a memory trace must be widely distributed since lesions do not have specific effects on memory traces (see [8]; for references see [10]). Because of the connections between neurons of different cell-assemblies, a network is formed.

For a cell-assembly it can be shown that a level of activation exists above which the activation will grow autonomously to its maximum level[11]. This property was also reported in [12-15] but within different frameworks. The introduction of the *critical threshold* in a conceptual network led to the hypothesis that the activation of a cell-assembly at a level below the critical threshold, corresponds – at the functional level – to a memory trace that is in a state of priming. Alternatively, a cell-assembly with an activation level above the critical threshold, corresponds to a memory trace that is 'in working memory'. Important implications of cell-assemblies and their critical threshold are discussed in [16, 17].

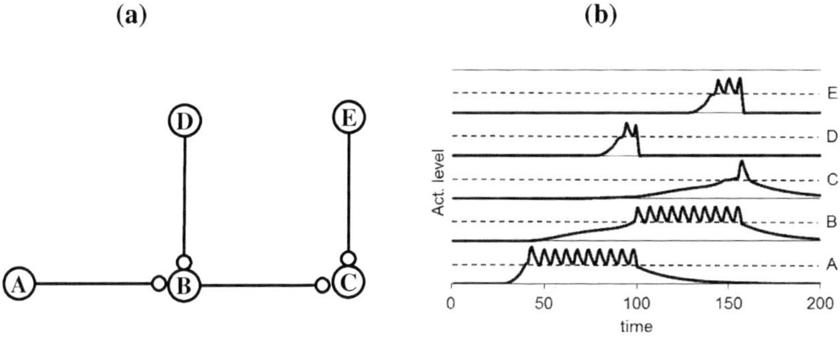

Fig. 2. (a) a large circle denotes a cell-assembly, a small circle a subpopulation of neurons of the adjacent cell-assembly, a line represents the permanent, bidirectional connections necessary for an excitation loop, (b) excitation curves for the propagation of excitation loops from assembly A to B and from B to C given coincident input from D, respectively E, dashed lines indicate the level of the critical threshold.

Coincidence of excitation loops. At the functional level an excitation loop in a conceptual network corresponds to the outcome of an information-processing step: something 'becomes known' in the network. This kind of information-processing event should produce a temporary equilibrium in the brain. In the model an excitation loop was chosen because it is the simplest mechanism to instantiate this equilibrium: a cell-assembly is active at a level above the critical threshold, and recurrent excitatory connections, together with inhibitory connections internal to a cell-assembly, ensure that the excitation level of the assembly starts to oscillate. Since information-processing proceeds in a more-or-less systematic way, excitation loops will have to do so, too. In a conceptual network this is accommodated by means of the following two assumptions[6,7]:

1. *Propagation.* Figure 2 illustrates the simulation of propagation of excitation loops from cell-assembly A to B, and then to C. Figure 2a shows that cell-assemblies A and D both have connections with cell-assembly B, whereas cell-assemblies B and E are both connected to cell-assembly C. The curve at the bottom of Figure 2b shows that, due to external activation, cell-assembly A starts to oscillate at a level above the critical threshold. Accordingly, an excitation loop from cell-assembly A in the direction of cell-assembly B occurs. This excitation loop alone is insufficient to cause a new excitation loop in cell-assembly B. However, B will enter a state of priming, since initially its activation level remains below the critical threshold. Only if a second excitation loop occurs, due to the external activation of cell-assembly D, both excitation loops will propagate to cell-assembly B, which will then become active above the critical threshold (see the corresponding excitation curve of cell-assemblies A, B, and D in Figure 2b). Accordingly, Figure 2 illustrates the idea of coincidence of excitation loops: A new excitation loop (in this case in cell-assembly B) only occurs if the cell-assembly involved receives simultaneous input from two other excitation loops (in this case from cell-assemblies A and D). Propagation of excitation loops can thus become selective. Similarly, excitation loops in cell-assemblies B and E leads to suprathreshold activation in cell-assembly C, where the propagation then stops. This propagation of excitation in a nctwork is similar to that of so-called synfire chains[18].
2. *Back-inhibition.* Once the concurrent excitation loops of two cell-assemblies have brought the activation level of a third cell-assembly above the level of the critical threshold, inhibitory connections of this cell-assembly (not shown in Figure 2a) extinguish the assemblies active in the two loops. This inhibitory mechanism is also present in the networks described in [13, 19]. Accordingly, the number of cell-assemblies active at a level above the critical threshold is limited by means of local interactions.

The simulations on which Figure 2 is based, and those in the rest of the paper, are carried out with networks in which each node is a cell-assembly and the links are the connections necessary for the propagation of excitation loops. A detailed description of the mechanisms involved in excitation loops and the simulation of their propagation is given in [5].

Binding and coincidence of activation. A strong theoretical argument for the existence of neural binding is the fact that we can immediately associate two arbitrary words[7]. If asked, we can reproduce one of them when given the other.

We cannot assume that the memory traces involved can activate each other directly because it is not plausible that permanent connections exist between them. Therefore, in the network a temporary connection must emerge: a temporary resonance enabled by an existing pathway and by means of which the two memory traces keep each other active. Accordingly, the simultaneous activation of two cell-assemblies in a conceptual network is a necessary condition for their binding. However, in the brain, more than two cell-assemblies are active together at any given moment. Therefore, another condition should exist that makes the two cell-assemblies for which a temporary pathway has to emerge, specific for a certain situation. In the proposed model this is the existence of a subnetwork of a conceptual network that activates both memory traces and that represents the actual context in which they play a role. At the structural level this activation ensures that the spike trains produced by the neurons of both cell-assemblies are 'in phase'. This phenomenon will be referred to as spike-resonance. If these conditions for the binding of two cell-assemblies occur, the temporary pathway necessary for their interaction emerges.

Learning. Within the model of a conceptual network, though not yet part of its simulations, binding can be considered as a precursor to learning[6,7]. If activation in a pair of temporarily connected memory traces persists, due to internal input (from other memory traces in the network) or input from the environment, their temporary binding gradually transforms into a permanent connection. At the structural level the transformation of temporary into permanent connections is carried by the aforementioned Tanzi-Hebb rule. The transformation process also affects the cell-assemblies involved. Dependent on the pattern of permanent connections formed, a cell-assembly may break up during learning and development. At the functional level, this corresponds to the emergence of new concepts in the network.

In order to account for learning, temporary connections have a strength which is dependent on the evolution of the activation levels of the two memory traces involved. In the model it is assumed that the initial strength of a temporary connection is therefore proportional to the levels of activation of these memory traces at the *moment of their binding*. Although the topic of learning itself is outside the scope of this paper, the strength of temporary connections does play a role in the model's account of letter- and word-recognition.

The actual context in the network changes rapidly as a consequence of the perpetual fluctuations in external or internal activation of the network. In the simulation programme this subnetwork is represented by means of so-called context lists. It is not possible to represent the spike resonance underlying the role of the context in the binding process at the level of a conceptual network. The spike resonance process refers to a lower level of description, which is not very suitable to represent cognitive tasks.

3. Why is Serial Binding Necessary?

The conditions in the aforementioned hypotheses on binding are limited to a single temporary binding. Therefore they are not sufficient for the binding necessary in word-processing, since for a single letter of a word there are already two excitation patterns: one for the identity of a letter and one for its location. The excitation patterns for identities and locations of the letters of a presented word, are all input simultaneously and belong to the same context. If the binding of identity and location of all letters of a word were to take place in parallel, this would draw heavily on the process of spike resonance. How many specific, robust, spike frequencies can be produced by the brain simultaneously with the effect that the correct identity-location pairs are formed?

Interference in spike resonance can be avoided if we make the assumption that binding takes place serially. In the network this is possible by means of a so-called scanning mechanism (see Figure 1). When the network is presented with a number of objects simultaneously, this mechanism transforms the corresponding external inputs into a series of excitation pairs, one per object. Each pair consists of an excitation pattern necessary for the representation of the identity, respectively the location of an object. The scanning mechanism then releases these excitation pairs into the network one after the other. The order in which the release of the pairs takes place, is dependent on the requirements of the task to be performed by the network. Therefore the part of a conceptual network representing the knowledge of tasks (the task network in Figure 1), triggers the scanning mechanism (see [5] for a detailed description of the scanning mechanism).

When the first excitation pair is released, this leads to the simultaneous occurrence of the excitation patterns for location and identity of the first letter of the presented word. Since these excitation patterns are then the only two in the current context, the hypothesized spike resonance does its work and a temporary connection between the two patterns emerges. Once this connection is formed, the second excitation pair is released. Accordingly, binding takes place in a rapid serial process, without the interference implied by parallel binding.

4. Representation of Identity and Location of Letters

It is important to distinguish the excitation patterns released in pairs by the scanning mechanism from the memory traces for the identity and location of letters in the network. As argued in the previous section, the memory trace for the identity of a letter is carried by a cell-assembly. This cell-assembly has developed in a cycle of perceptual-motor learning during which it became connected to related cell-assemblies. At the functional level, these cell-assemblies correspond to the memory traces of the motor-programs that enable the network to 'draw' or pronounce the letter. Due to these connections the memory trace for a certain letter becomes specific. It is assumed that if the excitation pair released by the scanning mechanism corresponds to a letter, the 'identity' excitation in the pair is one of many instances that activates the memory trace for that letter.

In a conceptual network, location is represented in a spatial map. It is assumed to be an inborn structure and plays an important role in the development of concepts. Unlike a cell-assembly, the spatial map does not represent identities. It is a neural structure in which excitation patterns can occur temporarily as a result of external activation of the network. The spatial map has the property that the spatial relationships of its excitation patterns are isomorphic to those of the external objects causing these excitation patterns. Accordingly, the spatial map represents pure form. This means that excitations are transient unless they become bound to a memory trace. For example, if certain excitation patterns in the spatial map, corresponding to one of the many forms of the letter 'A', become temporarily connected to the memory trace of the letter A, the memory trace may become active at a level above the critical threshold. At the functional level this would correspond to the awareness of the letter A at a certain location. If this memory trace is absent, or if the binding does not occur, the excitation patterns in the spatial map have no identity. They are only a transient spatial pattern, like those of matches having fallen out of their box. In the simulations of a conceptual network cited in this paper, a simplified map is used: a two-dimensional structure with nodes, representing possible locations.

5. Sequence Networks

In the processing of words, representation of sequence is essential. Within a framework of biologically plausible self-organisation, this representation must have its roots in evolution. In order to carry out the exploratory behaviour necessary for survival, organisms must be able to remember sequences, such as the successive loci of visual fixations or other goals of actions. In order to survive, it is necessary to be able to resume a sequence or a part of it. In the model it is therefore assumed that, early in ontogenetic development, neural structures emerge that represent sequence and that one of these structures develops into a general representation for sequence. In a conceptual network this structure will be referred to as a *global* sequence network. It contains memory traces for the concepts of rank order, *position nodes*, such as first, second, and third, and these can have temporary bindings with memory traces for arbitrary objects, including letters.

Because of the distributed nature of cell-assemblies, the temporary binding of position nodes to other memory traces should not be seen as being localized in a specific area of the cortex. Given the possible transformation of temporary connections into permanent ones, sequences can be learned all over the cortex. The functioning of the global sequence network is based on the propagation of excitation loops and on binding[5].

A crucial question in the study of the self-organisation of conceptual networks is how the global sequence network itself does develop or is learned. Knowledge of its final structure – as obtained from its role in letter- and word-processing, for example – poses important constraints on this process of self-organisation.

For the recognition of a word, however, one sequence network and its temporary binding to memory traces of letters is not sufficient. For the correct word representation to become active, the memory traces of its letters must satisfy a specific order. In a conceptual network, the order of the letters in each word is represented by means of position nodes in a *local* sequence network: a subnetwork similar to the global sequence network but specific for each word representation. Note that the term ‘local’ does not refer to a localised representation in the brain. A local sequence network activates the memory trace for the corresponding word by means of the coincidence of excitation loops, triggered by the global sequence network. In the present stage of development of the model, local sequence networks are hard-wired structures, as is the global sequence network. An important goal of future research is to show how they are produced by the aforementioned sequence learning. Like the global sequence network, a local sequence network therefore poses important constraints on the results of self-organising processes of learning.

6. Word-Recognition

Figure 3 displays the results of a computer simulation of the processing of a word in a conceptual network. The simulation addresses the first part of the central topic of this paper: the activation of a chunk by its elements. The figure describes the activation processes that take place after the discussed scanning

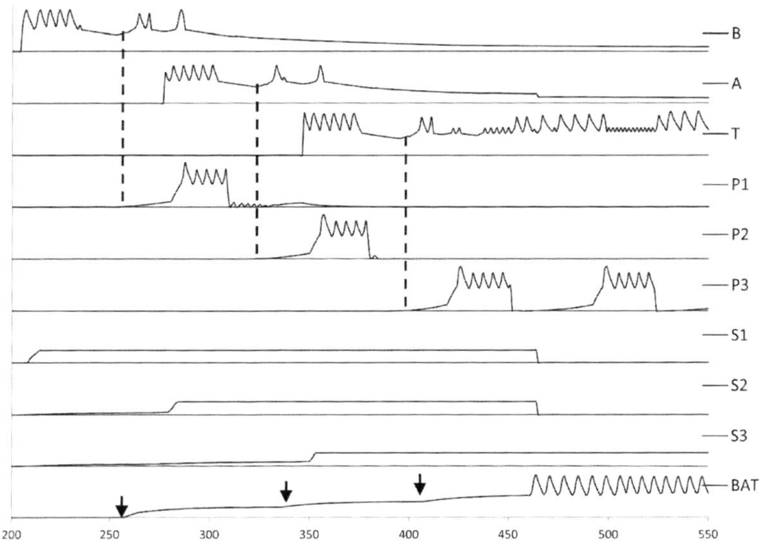

Fig. 3. Computer simulation of the processing of a word in a conceptual network. The horizontal axis gives the simulation time, the vertical axis the activation levels for the memory traces involved, the excitation peaks indicate oscillation of activation at a level above the critical threshold (see Figure 2): the memory traces for the letters B, A, and T, the position nodes in the global sequence network (P1..P3), respectively those in the local sequence network for the word BAT (S1..S3), as well as the activation level of the word representation itself. Vertical dotted lines indicate the moment of binding of letters to the position nodes of the global sequence network. The arrows indicate the excitation jumps due to coincidences of excitation loops in the position nodes of the local sequence network of the word BAT.

mechanism has been triggered by the task network. This means that when, for instance, the word 'bat' has been presented as input, the first excitation pair produced by the scanning mechanism leads to the activation of the memory trace for the letter 'b' and its location. The former is shown in the upper graph of Figure 3, where the peaks in the graph correspond to autonomous growth of activation above the level of the critical threshold. The activation of the location of the letter has a similar pattern in the spatial map (not shown in Figure 3). Both excitation patterns occur at the same time and are activated by the same context. Given the conditions for binding in the network, a temporary connection emerges between them. The occurrence of this binding triggers the global sequence network, as consequence of which position node P1 in the global sequence network, see Figure 3, becomes active. In the model, it is assumed that the activation of the global sequence network changes the subnetwork that represents the actual context in the network. This is necessary to create the context in which the memory trace for the letter 'b' is simultaneously active with position node P1. Accordingly, a temporary connection also emerges between these two excitation patterns. This is indicated in the upper left part of Figure 3 by means of a dotted line between the excitation curves of both memory traces. The line also marks their *moment of binding*.

Next, two fans of excitation loops burst out. Each fan consists of several excitation loops (see Figure 2) that have the same cell-assembly as their source. One fan originates in the global sequence network from the activated position node P1. The excitation loops in this fan activate, in parallel, the position nodes S1 in the local sequence networks of all word representations, among which position node S1 in the local sequence network of the word 'bat', see Figure 3. The source of the other fan of excitations is the memory trace of the newly bound letter, i.e. the letter 'b' in the given example. The excitation loops in this fan activate position nodes in the local sequence networks of word representations that correspond to occurrences of the letter 'b', irrespective of their positions in a word. In local sequence networks of certain word representations, there will now be a coincidence of excitation loops. These are the position nodes S1 in a local sequence network, that also receive excitation from the memory trace of the letter 'b'.

As a result of coincidences of excitation loops, the excitation levels of the memory traces for words starting with a 'b' increase. For the remaining letters of the presented word a similar process takes place. This results in three excitation jumps of the activation level of the word node 'bat', as indicated by the arrows in the graph at the bottom of Figure 3. The excitation fans resulting from the binding of the last letter then create a coincidence of activation in the last position node in the local sequence network of this word node. This event pushes word node's activation level over the critical threshold. At a functional level, it corresponds to the subjective experience of reading a word in a single glance, which is one interpretation of the word-superiority effect[1]. At the structural level, however, a rapid, partly serial process is the neural substrate of this experience, according to the chosen model.

If a string of presented letters only forms part of a word, or if letter order is incorrect, several memory traces for words become active but all at a level below the critical threshold. The distance between their activation level and the threshold, determines the extent to which these memory traces are primed. Alternatively, if the letters of a word are scrambled, the activation level of the memory trace of the original word may still reach the critical threshold. This happens when the memory trace is primed by the context in which the scrambled word is presented. Accordingly, it can be explained why an experienced reader is able to recognize an incorrectly spelled word. This recognition is facilitated when the first and last letter of the word have kept their position. In the model this is accounted for by the special role of the binding of the memory traces for the first and the last letter to the position nodes in the global sequence network: the initialisation, respectively finalization of the word-recognition process displayed in Figure 3.

7. Letter Identification

Word-recognition is an example of chunking in the sense that a number of elements is recognized as a whole. The chosen representations for words, letters, and sequence, however, can be generalized to other tasks, notably those referring to the second part of the central topic of this paper: the identification of a letter at a given target position in a presented word.

The recognition of a word and the subsequent identification of one of its letters impose different requirements on the network. During word recognition, a very rapid, 'ballistic' propagation of excitation loops takes place from the position node for the first letter to that of the last. This fast process is triggered by a scanning mechanism that seriates the input and thus creates the conditions for robust binding.

From a viewpoint of self-organisation, subsequent letter identification requires that the same global sequence network becomes active. To assume the existence of a second global sequence network that would 'read-out' the first one, is neither a plausible, nor a parsimonious argument. As we argued in the beginning of this paper, each change of a self-organising system has to work with that which is already there. For that reason it is plausible that the same global sequence network is involved in the perceptual stage of the task (word-recognition) as well as in the response stage (letter identification). This is also a more parsimonious account: It results in a simpler network. For future research, the argument also constrains the process of self-organisation by means of which the network should develop and learn.

However, the mode of operation of the global sequence network during letter identification must be different from that during word recognition. Each time a position node in the global sequence network becomes active above the critical threshold, the propagation of excitation loops must be temporarily interrupted. At the functional level, this interruption corresponds to the test of whether the target position of the identification task is reached. At the structural level, the interruption is carried by the mechanism of coincidence of excitation loops, discussed before. A complete description of the 'controlled' operation mode of the global sequence network is described in [5], but would go beyond the scope of this paper.

When the excitation loops propagate through the global sequence network during letter identification, position nodes become active successively at a level above the critical threshold. In turn, each position node activates the letter node it is temporarily connected with. Accordingly, temporary connections that come into existence during word-recognition later play a fundamental role as re-entrant pathways[20] in the identification of letter. When the propagation of excitation loops reaches the position node corresponding to the target position, the letter node activated by this position node becomes temporarily connected to a memory trace that in the task corresponds to the letter to be identified. This binding effectuates the actual response in the performance of the task[7].

The quality of the task performance depends on the strength of the temporary connections. In the model, and in line with the chosen principles of self-organisation, it is assumed that the strength of a temporary connection between two memory traces is proportional to the activation levels of both nodes at their *moment of binding*. The strength of the temporary connections between the position nodes of the global sequence network and the letter nodes of a presented word are therefore determined during word-recognition. Since the activation level of a position node in the global sequence network is assumed to be equal for each moment of binding, the strength of a temporary connection will depend on the activation level of the involved letter node. In the simulation shown in Figure 3 the presented word caused a strong activation of the letter nodes, since in all nodes the activation level exceeded the critical threshold. Accordingly, the temporary connections that emerge all have their maximal strength, which leads to an optimal performance.

External activation need not activate letter nodes to a level above the critical threshold. This happens, for example, when a word is only briefly presented. In these cases, the network's performance on a letter identification task is determined by the following processes:

Decay. The activation of letter nodes decays during the scanning process and before they become temporarily bound to the spatial map and global sequence network. The effect of this decay increases with position.
Position-specific top-down activation. Due to coincidences of activation in the position nodes in the local sequence networks of word nodes, letter nodes receive top-down activation. Because of the successive activation of these position nodes, see Figure 3, this activation is position specific.
Reverberation. When excitation loops propagate through the global sequence network during word recognition, a reverberation occurs at the last position node. Instead of a quick succession from one position node to the next, the excitation reverberates between the memory trace for the last letter and the last position node in the global sequence network, as can be seen in Figure 3. Due to this reverberation the strength of the last temporary connection will be relatively strong.

8. Conclusion

We have seen how the process of letter- and word-recognition can be given a representation based on self-organisation. The model's predictions can be tested in several types of experiments. In experiments on masked priming[1], for example, the addition of letters to a prime may jeopardize binding. For example, a prime consisting of only the end letters of a target word should have more effect than a prime consisting of the end letters preceded by a number neutral 'filler' letters, not occurring in the target but giving prime and target an equal length. According to the model, the binding process induced by a prime of the former type (only end letters) still produces some partial coincidences of activation in the local sequence network of the word node for the target. This word node will therefore become primed. A prime of the latter type, however, consists of more letters than one consisting of end letters only. It is then assumed that the exposure time of the prime does not allow the serial binding to finish in time. As a consequence, priming is less strong or even absent because the binding for the end letters, necessary for the priming effect to occur, does not take place.

Another series of experiments that are currently being worked out, focuses on tasks in which the *n*-th letter has to be identified in words and non-words. These letter sequences are presented briefly (50 msec). The binding process and the resulting activation of word representations will therefore also be disturbed. Given the model's assumptions on the serial nature of binding, a decrease in task performance with an increase of the target position will be expected, with an exception for the last letter of a (non)word. Due to the assumed position-specific top-down activation, the decrease in performance over positions will be less for words than for non-words. These last studies are similar to the classic experiments on word-superiority[3,4]. However, as far as the author knows, neither the hypothesized sequence effects nor the aforementioned effects of masked priming have been reported in the literature yet.

We have presented a line of arguments that starts with the Tanzi-Hebb learning rule and ends with new predictions on letter- and word-recognition. The learning rule is necessary for the formation of the nodes and permanent connections of a conceptual network. We have argued that also temporary connections are required and that the binding involved is re-entrant and serial in nature. Because of these properties this model can be used to explain the recognition of words as well as the identification of letters within a word. In addition, the construction of the model is based on principles of self-organisation. Accordingly, it contains structures that are likely to emerge in the autonomous development of a biologically plausible, cognitive system: the global sequence network and its local counterparts. Knowledge of the functioning of these structures in their final state, based on the selective propagation of excitation loops, is essential to future simulation studies on the actual, bottom-up self-organisation of conceptual networks.

Acknowledgments

The author is grateful to G.J. Dalenoort and two anonymous reviewers for comments on an earlier version of this paper.

References

1. J. Grainger, "Cracking the orthographic code: An introduction," *Language and Cognitive Processes,* vol. **23**, pp. 1-35, 01, 2008.
2. C. von der Malsburg, "The what and why of binding: The modeler's perspective," *Neuron,* vol. **24**, pp. 95-104, 1999.
3. J. McClelland and D. Rumelhart, "An interactive activation model of context effects in letter perception: I. An account of basic findings," *Psychological Review,* vol. **88**, pp. 375-407, 1981.
4. D. Rumelhart and J. McClelland, "An interactive activation model of context effects in letter perception: II. The contextual enhancement effect and some tests and extensions of the model," *Psych. Rev.,* vol. **89**, pp. 60-94, 1982.

5. P. H. de Vries, "The Implications of Self-organisation for Models of Letter- and Word-Recognition," *In preparation, available upon request to the author,* 2015.
6. P. H. de Vries and G. J. Dalenoort, "The implication of binding for models of cognitive brain function," in *Proc. 7th Neural Comp. and Psy. Workshop: Connectionist Models of Cognition and Perception*, J. A. Bullinaria and W. Lowe, Eds. Singapore: World Scientific, 2002, pp. 14-23.
7. P. H. de Vries, "Effects of binding in the identification of objects," *Psychological Research,* vol. **1**, pp. 41-66, 12, 2004.
8. D. O. Hebb, *The Organization of Behavior.* New York: Wiley, 1949.
9. E. Tanzi, "I fatti e le induzione nell'odierna istologia del sistema nervoso," *Rivista Sperimentale Di Freniatria,* vol. **19**, pp. 419-472, 1893.
10. K. S. Lashley, "In search of the engram," *Symposia of the Society of Experimental Biology,* vol. **4**, pp. 454-482, 1951.
11. G. J. Dalenoort, "The representation of tasks in active cognitive networks," *Cognitive Systems,* vol. **1**, pp. 253-272, 1985.
12. V. Braitenberg, "Cell assemblies in the cerebral cortex," in *Theoretical Approaches to Complex Systems*, R. Heim and G. Palm, Eds. Berlin: Springer, 1978, pp. 171-188.
13. D. G. MacKay, *The Organization of Perception and Action: A Theory for Language and Other Cognitive Skills.* New York: Springer, 1987.
14. C. R. Huyck, "Creating hierarchical categories using cell assemblies," *Connect. Sci.,* vol. **19**, pp. 1-24, 2007.
15. C. T. Kello, "Critical Branching Neural Networks," *Psychol. Rev.,* vol. **120**, pp. 230-254, 2013.
16. P. H. de Vries and K. R. van Slochteren, "The nature of the memory trace and its neurocomputational implications," *J. Comput. Neurosci.,* vol. **25**, pp. 188-202, 2008.
17. M. Garagnani, Y. Shtyrov and F. Pulvermüller, "Effects of attention on what is known and what is not: MEG evidence for functionally discrete memory circuits," *Frontiers in Human Neuroscience,* vol. **3**, pp. 1-12, 2009.
18. M. Abeles, G. Hayon and D. Lehmann, "Modeling compositionality by dynamic binding of synfire chains," *J. Comput. Neurosci.,* vol. **17**, pp. 179-201, 2004.
19. K. Fukushima, "Neocognitron - a Self-Organizing Neural Network Model for a Mechanism of Pattern-Recognition Unaffected by Shift in Position," *Biol. Cybern.,* vol. **36**, pp. 193-202, 1980, 1980.
20. G. Edelman, "Neural Darwinism - Selection and Reentrant Signaling in Higher Brain-Function," *Neuron,* vol. **10**, pp. 115-125, 1993.

Learning Bidirectional Connections Between Areas With Standard Spike-Timing-Dependent Plasticity

M. Klein*, A. Cangelosi, and T. Wennekers
Centre for Robotics and Neural Systems, Plymouth University,
Portland Square, Plymouth PL4 8AA, UK
**E-mail: michael.q.klein@gmail.com*
www.plymouth.ac.uk

Spike-timing-dependent plasticity (STDP) is a learning algorithm that is simple, biologically plausible, and powerful. Hence, one would expect STDP (likely in combination with other learning algorithms) to be a key component in cortical models of higher cognitive functions, such as language comprehension or production. Such models would need to involve multiple brain areas and bidirectional links between representations in those different areas. However, STDP is an asymmetrical learning algorithm (in contrast to classical Hebbian learning, which is symmetrical). This makes the acquisition of bilateral connections between two neurons almost impossible and bilateral connections between representations very challenging. Here, we propose a solution based on specific connectivity patterns. Then, using numerical simulations, we show that our approach allows STDP to create strong bidirectional links between representations. Finally, we compare our architecture to neuroanatomical data.

Keywords: spike-timing-dependent plasticity; STDP; Hebbian learning; unsupervised learning; cortex; bilateral connections.

1. Introduction

It would be vastly inefficient for the brain to use a completely different set of representations for language production and language comprehension. Under the assumption that word *meaning* is represented somewhere in the brain (localised or distributed) and word *forms* are represented somewhere else in the brain (perhaps as some form of auditory-motor patterns), we can deduct that these two types of representations must have some sort of two-way connection. The reason is: not only must a word be able to activate its meaning (in language comprehension), but meaning must also be able to activate an appropriate word (in language production). This principle is illustrated in Seidenberg and McClelland's *triangular model*[1] and Plaut and Kello's model of phonology[2]. These classic connectionist models have great value in understanding distributed cognitive processing and the relation between neural processing and psycholinguistics. However, the flood of functional imaging data on language processing might, at this point, benefit significantly from explanatory models that take more neuroanatomical constraints into account. The increased understanding of physiological mechanisms of learning in the brain[3,4] would allow such models to use biologically plausible learning rules. Also, the increased computational power made available by highly parallel neuromorphic hardware such as SpiNNaker[5] is predicted to allow neural models with up to 1 billion spiking neurons to run in real time in the near future. Hence, modelling language processing in the brain with computational units that correspond to the single neuron in the real brain moves within the realm of possibilities.

Most language processing has been demonstrated to take place in the cerebral cortex[6]. There is convincing evidence that connections in the cerebral cortex are formed by unsupervised learning of the Hebbian[7] type. STDP, being a form of Hebbian learning for spiking neurons, is increasingly well established as at least one of the learning rules of the cortex[4,8]. Hence, it would be a strong candidate for the learning rule of such a model. *Standard* STDP, however, has the well established problem of not being able to create bilateral connections between two neurons[9,10].

This is due to the very nature of STDP. If two neurons have synapses in both directions, any event that will potentiate the synapses in one direction will depress the synapse in the other direction (as will be explained in more detail in section 3). While it is possible to change parameters of the standard learning rules, specifically to increase the strength of potentiation so that it grossly out-weights the strength of depression, such a change will lead to an undesired increase of most weights, leading to strong links between every neuron in the long run. Therefore, to assure long-term stability of firing rates, parameters in standard STDP rules are typically chosen such that inhibition slightly dominates excitation[11].

There are, however, non-standard forms of STDP obtained by modifying the STDP learning rule. One of those has been demonstrated to allow the establishment of bilateral connections at high firing rates, while at low firing rates only unilateral connections are established[10]. We estimated that this approach is likely to be problematic in multi-area models where intermediate layers have no direct external input. Too high frequencies in those areas might lead to uncontrolled associations of neurons with all other neurons. Therefore, we would like to introduce an approach that uses the more established (frequency independent) standard STDP learning rule.

We propose an architecture that allows patterns to be associated between two brain areas by using sparse area to area connections. Hence, while representations in different brain areas are connected in both directions, hardly any pairs of neurons are. To completely activate representational patterns of an area recurrent within-area connections are used. Note that once a multi-layer assembly is learned, single spikes can nevertheless travel quickly through the layers for fast-forward visual recognition[12]. The recurrent connections are then only needed to reactivate the complete assembly.

2. Spike-Timing Dependent Plasticity

Within the last decade, research on STDP has grown several theoretical branches. In general, the proposed plasticity rules share the feature that the weight changes are dependent on the temporal relation between the pre- and the post-synaptic spikes, specifically: the weight increases when the pre-synaptic spike precedes the post-synaptic spike and decreases if the post-synaptic spike precedes the pre-synaptic spike (although the opposite has been proposed as well). The closer the two spikes are in time, the stronger the increase or decrease of the weight.

They differ mainly along two dimensions: The first dimension is the way the weight change is (or is not) dependent on the current weight. This dependence can be additive[8] as in standard STDP, multiplicative[13] or exponential[14]. The second dimension is which pairs (or even triplets[10]) contribute to plasticity. The most prominent types of pairing being *all-to-all*[15] and *nearest neighbour*[16]. *All-to-all* means that in case of a spike event, the STDP learning rule is applied to that event in relation to all previous spiking events. Of course, a post-synaptic spike is only paired with all pre-synaptic spikes and a pre-synaptic spike is only paired with all post-synaptic spikes. *Nearest neighbour* means that the spike event is only paired with the last preceding spike.

The simulations reported in this paper are all based on what one may call *standard* STPD learning rule[8], i.e., additive weight dependence, and all-to-all spike pairing. Therefore, weight change Δw is calculated with equation 1.

$$\Delta w = \begin{cases} A_{+}exp(\Delta t/\tau_{+}) & \text{if } \Delta t < 0 \\ -A_{-}exp(-\Delta t/\tau_{-}) & \text{if } \Delta t \geq 0 \end{cases} \tag{1}$$

Here A_+ and $-A_-$ are the learning rates for depression and excitation, respectively. Since this is standard additive STPD this learning rate is not dependent on the previous weight in any way. Hence, unless the weight has an upper and lower bound, it can grow or decrease indefinitely. In our simulation, the upper limit of the weight is 1 and the lower limit is 0.

3. Difficulty of Creating Bilateral Connections with STDP

Note that when we talk about the difficulty in the formation of bilateral connections between two neurons, we do not talk about whether or not there are synapses in both directions, but about the weight of any synapses present. STDP makes it close to impossible to develop significantly strong excitatory weights in both directions. This is because STDP is basically a mechanism for detecting causality. If a neuron A fires before a neuron B the synapse connecting A to B is potentiated. The synapse has learned that the event E_A that caused A to fire preceded the event E_B that caused B to fire. The strength of the STDP learning rule is that it detects such a repetitive directed sequence of events. Note, however, that whenever A fires before B and the weight W_{AB} is potentiated, B also fires after A and the weight W_{BA} is depressed. This means that, if STDP is used as a learning algorithm and we have two neurons with synapses in both directions, only one synapse can develop a strong weight, while the other will be depressed.

There is, however, a parameter called the α-parameter which determines the relation between the weight increase and the weight decrease. It is defined in equation 2.

$$\alpha = \frac{A_- \tau_-}{A_+ \tau_+} \tag{2}$$

If the α parameter is set to a value greater than 1, the weights tend to go down, in particular if the firing of the pre- and post-synaptic neuron is random (noise)[11]. If the α parameter is set to a value smaller than 1, weights tend to increase. Hence, it is possible to set the α parameter of standard STDP to a value, in which the strength of potentiation in both directions grossly out-weights the strength of depression. In this way, strong bidirectional links can be formed between two neurons. Such a change, however, will in the long run lead to an undesired increase of most weights, leading to strong links between all neurons in the model. It can, therefore, be ruled out as a solution.

4. Our Approach

We have established that under a reasonable parameter setting, strong bilateral connections between two neurons cannot be established in a model that learns with standard STDP. However, it would of course be possible to connect two brain areas using two distinct hidden layers, as shown in Fig. 1A.

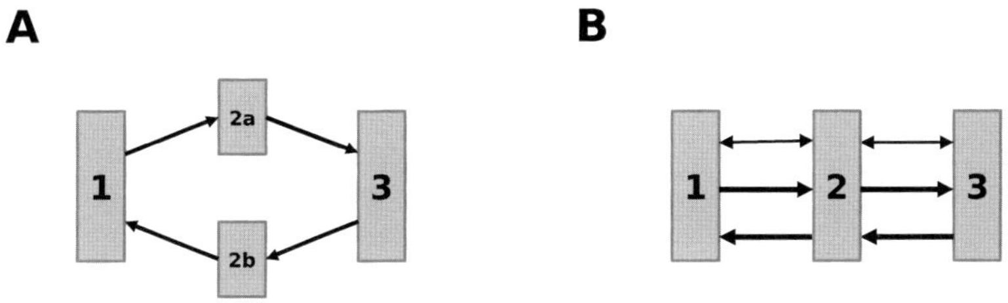

Fig. 1. A: If the intermediate layer is split into two *zones* 2a and 2b, then bilateral connections between two neurons would not be necessary to connect the two areas 1 and 3. B: Sparse probabilistic connections between areas lead to few bilaterally connected neuron pairs and many unilateral connections.

While this is certainly a valid way of connecting brain areas (and is definitely worth further exploration), two distinct hidden layers are needed. The key feature of such an architecture is the following: The outward connection of a neuron (the connection going to the next area) go to a different neuron than the inward connections (the connection coming from the next area). Consequently, there are no direct bidirectional links between neurons of one area with neurons of the other area.

This property can be approximated without the need for two distinct hidden layers by the usage of probabilistic sparse connections between two areas. If the connections are sparse and the probability of connections is symmetrical (i.e., the same probability in both directions), the chance of bidirectional synaptic links between neurons decreases faster than the probability of the connection in one direction (see Fig. 1B). This means that the number of connections in one direction can still be fairly high, while the percentage of connections that are bidirectional is very small.

This is computed in the following manner: with a connection probability of p_{sym} of a neuron n_A in area A to project to a neuron in area B and the same probability of a neuron n_B in area B to project to a neuron in area A, the probability of neurons n_A and n_B to have a direct bilateral connection is p_{sym}^2. Consequently, the probability of having a unilateral connection in only one (but any) direction is $p_{sym} * (1 - p_{sym}) + p_{sym} * (1 - p_{sym})$, which is the sum of the probabilities of being connected in one, but not in the other direction. For example, if area A is connected to area B with $p = 0.25$ and area B is connected to area A with the same probability, then the probability of two neurons of these two brain areas to be bilaterally connected is only $p = 0.06$, while the probability of two neurons to be connected unilaterally is $p = 0.38$ (0.19 upwards and 0.19 downwards). Fig. 2 shows the relation between symmetrical probability and the probability of bilateral connections.

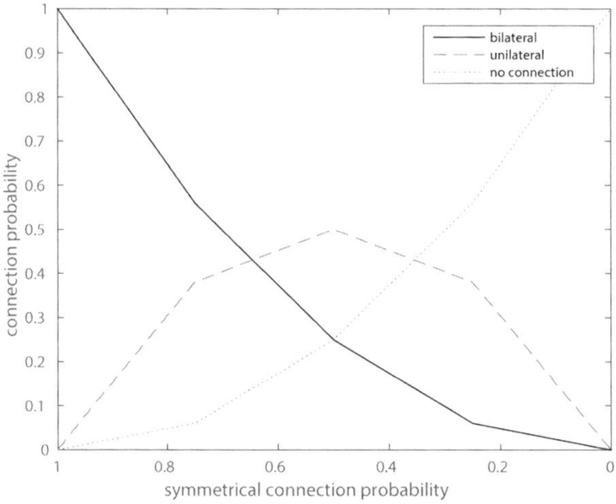

Fig. 2. Effect of symmetric probability of connections on probability of bilaterally connected neuron pairs. If two areas are connected with a symmetrical probability in both directions the probability of bilateral connections between two neurons (one in each area) decreases very fast. When the symmetrical probability is in the mid to low range, the probability of bilateral connection is very low, while there are still sufficient unilateral connections. Note that x-axis of the graph runs from 1 to 0.

Hence, we can connect two brain areas bilaterally while almost no pairs of neurons have bilateral synaptic links. Of course, as a consequence of having very sparse area to area connections, the patterns need to be completed using recurrent connections within the area. If sufficient neurons of a pattern are activated in the area by connections from outside the area, the pattern can be completed using the recurrent connections within the area.

5. Simulations

5.1. *Architecture*

While this approach does not need a hidden layer, models that use one are known to be more powerful. Hence, we ran our simulations using a three area model. Two of these areas receive outside input (henceforth called *input areas* or areas 1 and 3), while one area does not (the *hidden area* or area 2). Every area consists of a population of 625 excitatory neurons and a population of 625 inhibitory neurons. The function of the inhibitory neurons is homeostatic. They balance the overall activity. Using a more realistic ratio of excitatory to inhibitory cells[17] (which is known to be close to 4:1) would simply lead to higher inhibitory weights from the inhibitory to the excitatory population. Also, the combination of excitatory and inhibitory neurons within an area is know to lead to oscillations[18], which in turn stabilises the patterns within an area by means of recurrent connections. Therefore, every excitatory population has excitatory connections to the inhibitory populations, which in turn project back to the excitatory population of the same area. The excitatory neurons also have connections with the other excitatory neurons in the same area (recurrent connections). The probability of recurrent connections was held constant at $p = 0.95$ for this study.

Only excitatory layers have connections to other areas. We ran 10 simulations for each probability of layer-to-layer connectivity in this set:

$$P = \{0.01, 0.03, 0.05, 0.10, 0.15, 0.20, 0.25, \ldots 1.00\} \tag{3}$$

5.2. *Neuron Model*

We used current-based leaky integrate-and-fire neurons, with membrane potential v, the dynamics of which is given in equation 4.

$$\frac{dv}{dt} = -\frac{v}{\tau_m} + I\frac{1}{C} \tag{4}$$

Here, τ_m is the membrane time constant, C is the capacitance of the membrane and I is the input current to the neuron. The input I to the neuron, caused by an incoming spike from another neuron is computed with an alpha function (equation 5).

$$I_s(t) = w\frac{e}{\tau_\alpha}te^{-t/\tau_\alpha} \tag{5}$$

Here, w is the weight (or peak value) and τ_α is the synaptic rise time.

A spike is emitted once the membrane potential v of the neuron reaches the threshold θ. Afterwards, the membrane potential remains at reset potential for an (absolute) refractory period of $0.5ms$.

5.3. *Training and Testing*

The models in our study were trained using pairs of patterns to the input areas of the model. Each pattern pair was presented 200 times for 1 second with 1 second break in between. The patterns were presented by means of Poisson neurons connected to the input areas spiking with a frequency of 80Hz. The patterns consisted of 625-dimensional random bit patterns. The percentage of bits that were set to one was 3%. Patterns were completely orthogonal. Random white noise with a frequency of 2 Hz is presented to all excitatory neurons of all areas at all times.

After training, the pattern is presented to area 1 only and we tested the reconstruction of the corresponding pattern in area 3. If the spiking activity of a neuron is above a threshold it is considered to be activated by the pattern in area 1. Neurons that are part of the pattern and are not activated are considered to be errors. The same holds for neurons that are activated, but are not part of the pattern.

5.4. *Results*

As expected, we found oscillation in all brain areas around 40Hz. These are caused by the interaction between the excitatory and the inhibitory layer (see Fig. 3). The excitatory connections (both between and within a layer) drive the activation up until the inhibitory neurons go above threshold which drives the activity down again. Once the activity is low, the inhibitory neurons no longer fire, which allows the excitatory neurons to drive the activation up again.

The representations in the middle layer (which are not determined by external input), gradually emerges (visible in Fig. 3C and D).

In simulations that used a high connection probability, bilateral connections between the patterns in the two input areas was not established.

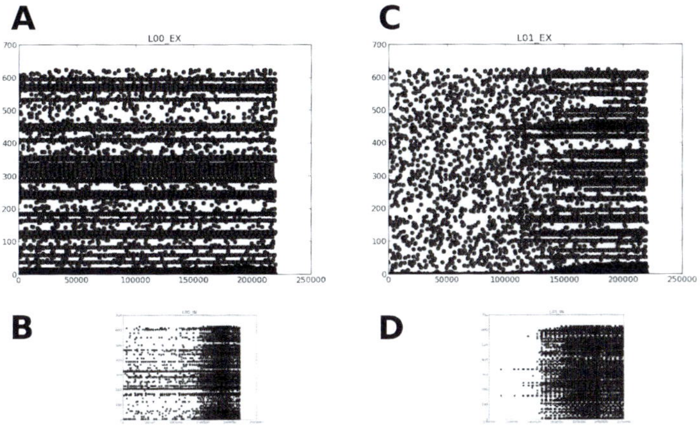

Fig. 3. A spike plot of the excitatory layer (A) and inhibitory layer (B) of one input layer. layer, as well as the excitatory layer (C) and inhibitory layer (D) of the hidden layer.

During the testing period, when the pattern was no longer applied to area 3, the pattern dissolves and a new, completely unrelated pattern emerges (visible in Fig. 4).

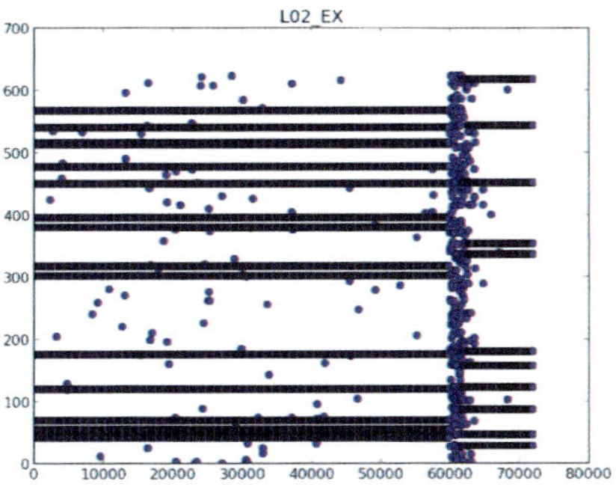

Fig. 4. A spike plot of area 3.

This can be explained by the weight patterns that emerge during training (Fig. 5). The Hinton-diagram shows weights of a neuron in the middle layer to layer 3. This neuron is connected to the input pattern in layer 1 by strong connections. If the connections had been established as desired, it would show strong links to the desired pattern in the next layer. Instead in shows exactly the opposite pattern. The weights that should be the strongest are in fact the weakest.

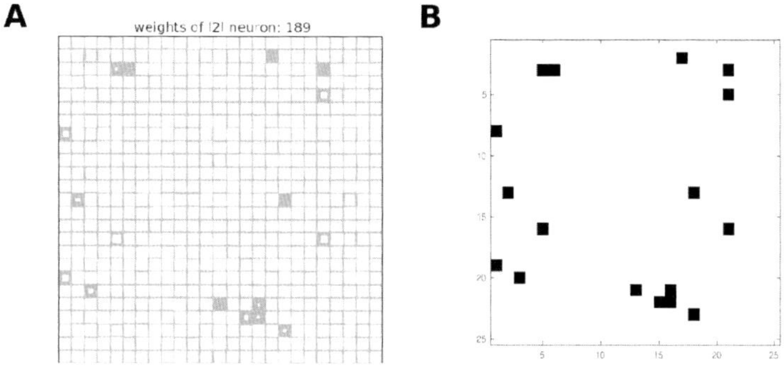

Fig. 5. (A) a Hinton-diagram (i.e., the weights in a matrix of white squares, where the size of the square represents the strength of the weight) of a neuron in the middle layer. (B) The target pattern that this neuron should activate. The weights show the opposite of the desired configuration.

As already sketched in section 3, this is happening because when the pattern is applied to area 3, it generates a random pattern in hidden area 2 and connects with it with strong weights. While the connection in this direction grows stronger, the corresponding connections in the other directions grow weaker. When training stops, a strong link has been established from the patterns in area 3 to area 2, but no such link exists in the other direction (area 2 to area 3). Hence, during testing, the activation of a pattern in area 1 can activate a pattern in the hidden area, but no activation of the trained pattern in area 3 is possible from there.

While this finding agrees with our theoretical predictions, the more important result of this study is the behaviour of those models that had sparse between-area connections. For such a parameter setting, we found that bilateral connections between brain areas can indeed be learned with STDP. In contrast to the case reported above, the pattern was reconstructed through the learned weights, once the external stimulation was switched off. The simulations showed that (with the parameters used in this study) the performance peaks between $p = 0.05$ and $p = 0.10$, being completely error free (see Fig. 6). The error reaches ceiling at $p = 0.35$. This is because of the way the error is computed. To decide whether a neuron is part of an assembly the neuron with the highest firing frequency is detected and all neurons that fire within a certain percentile of that frequency are considered active. This works well unless there is no active assembly, because then all neurons are considered part of the assembly and therefore the error reaches maximum.

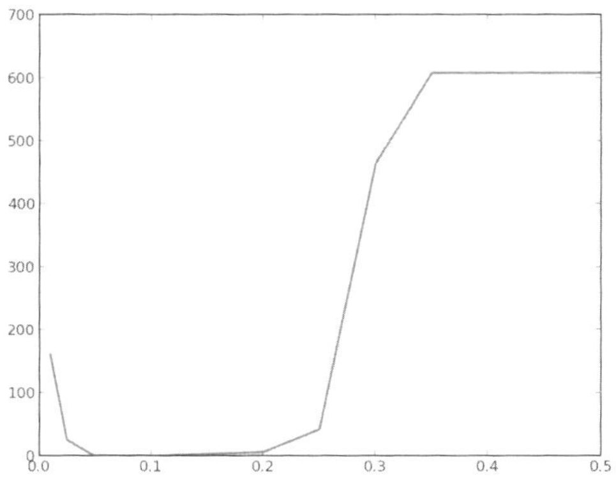

Fig. 6. The image shows the optimal connection probability (with other parameters being fixed).

We also tested the possibility of this architecture to form strong bilateral links between brain areas for 4, 5, and 6 area models. Pattern association was observed over multiple areas with a slight drop in performance for more layers. This will be reported in more detail elsewhere.

Given the small network size of the model used in the simulations, bilateral multi-area pattern association is limited to 3 patterns. Trying to learn more patterns lead to a fusion of patterns into one big neuron cluster. This is probably due to connections between the neurons of one patterns and neurons of the other patterns being potentiated by noise. Once the connections are above a certain threshold, they cannot be depressed anymore because any pre-synaptic spike leads to a postsynaptic spike, which causes the weight to increase until it reaches maximum. As soon as two patterns are connected by one strong synapse, they will co-activate and therefore all the neurons of one pattern will form strong synaptic links to the neurons of the other pattern.

6. Discussion

Our simulations clearly show that learning bi-directional associations between patterns in different brain areas is possible with standard STDP. However, it requires sparse area-to-area connectivity (5-10%). High recurrent within-area connectivity is needed to ensure pattern completion.

To compare these connectivity specifications with connectivity in the real brain is not straightforward, since there is no clear data about the percentage of neurons in one area that connect to another area. There are, however, a number of studies on this and closely related topics.

In a tracer study in the mouse Schüz et al.[19] finds that 55 to 70% of the stained axons were located in the near field of the neuron. Under the assumption that the density of synapses is constant along the axons, we can deduct that 55 to 70% of a neurons projections are inside the area. According to Schüz and Braitenberg[20], the vast number of cortico-cortical fibres project to areas within the same lobe or to neighbouring areas in a different lobe, with the number of fibres of a certain length being inversely proportional to their length and no more than 2% going into the intra-hemispheric long-range bundle. Hence, the 30 to 45% of the synapses that are going to another brain area are distributed among all brain areas these neurons project to. Taking this data into account, a very low connection probability between areas and a high connection probability within areas seems biologically very realistic.

In terms of actual numbers of connections, Braitenberg and Schüz[17] estimate $9.2 \times 10^4/mm^3$ neurons and $7.2 \times 10^8/mm^3$ synapses in mouse cortex resulting in a ratio of 1:7826. Note that this does not mean that all synapses in that area are between neurons in that area, but it does give a good indication of the very high number of actually synapses per neuron. However, given that we have only 1250 neurons per brain area, we can certainly not model 7825 synapses per neuron.

One important aspect of our model that we like to point out is the within-area interaction between excitatory and inhibitory neurons. Not only does this keep the overall spiking activity in balance, but it also generates oscillations. These oscillations have the effect that at the input layers, the patterns can be applied to the model using Poisson neurons. No precise timing of the patterns are necessary. The oscillations naturally bring about the synchronous activation of neurons necessary for learning to the patterns. This is of the essence for the hidden layer where no external input can be used to control the timing.

It is possible that varying time delays[21] could also enable bidirectional communication between brain areas. In the real brain, there are time delays between spike events and post-synaptic potentials and these delays differ between individual connections. If two neurons are connected using a different timing, it might no longer be the case that every time the synapse in one direction is potentiated by STDP, the synapse in the opposite direction is depressed. The variation of delays is likely to be higher in long range connections between areas. Hence, it is worth studying time delays as a possible solution to the problem of bilateral association between different brain areas.

Also, it has to be said that the cortex is laminar and contains interlaminar and intra-laminar circuitry. Therefore, it is not likely that the bidirectional connections between areas are directly between the same neurons. Instead, they might use a type a relay station, similar to the approach we have mentioned above, but have not pursued it in the simulation studies reported here. In the brain there is a difference between feed-forward and feed-back connections[22], while in our simulations both directions have the same architecture. For a more realistic biological model, a difference between feed-back and feed-forward connections should be taken into account. One difference could be (and this is just speculation at this point) that the feed-back connections use a relay station. Consequently, feed-forward connections would be direct (and fast), while the feed-back connections would be poly-synaptic (and slower). The problem of direct bidirectional connections would not occur.

In this paper, we demonstrated that a documented difficulty of standard STDP can be solved without modifying the learning rule by an interaction of architectural considerations. It remains to be tested how far this approach scales up or generalises. Nevertheless, this research has solved a difficult problem and made an important step on the way to more complex STDP-based architectures and brought us closer to models of higher cognitive functions and language processing.

Acknowledgements

This work was supported under EPSRC Grant EP/J004561/1 (BABEL). We would like to thank two anonymous reviewers for very constructive comments.

References

1. M. S. Seidenberg and J. L. McClelland, A distributed, developmental model of word recognition and naming, *Psychological Review* **96**, 523 (1989).
2. D. C. Plaut and C. T. Kello, The emergence of phonology from the interplay of speech comprehension and production: A distributed connectionist approach, in *The emergence of language*, ed. B. MacWhinney (Mahwah, NJ: Erlbaum, 1999) pp. 381–415.
3. G. Q. Bi and M. M. Poo, Synaptic modifications in cultured hippocampal neurons: dependence on spike timing, synaptic strength, and postsynaptic cell type, *J. Neurosci.* **18**, 10464 (1998).
4. W. G. H. Markram and P. J. Sjöström, A history of spike-timing-dependent plasticity, *Frontiers in Synaptic Neuroscience* **3**, 1 (2011).
5. X. Jin, M. Lujan, L. A. Plana, S. Davies, S. Temple and S. Furber, Modeling spiking neural networks on spinnaker, *Computing in Science & Engineering* **12** (2010).
6. P. Indefrey and W. J. M. Levelt, The neural correlates of language production, in *The New Cognitive Neurosciences*, ed. M. Gazzaniga (Cambridge, MA: MIT Press, 2000) pp. 845–865, 2nd edn.
7. D. O. Hebb, *The Organization of Behaviour* (Wiley New York, 1949).
8. S. Song, K. D. Miller and L. F. Abbott, Competitive Hebbian learning through spike-timing dependent synaptic plasticity, *Nature Neuroscience* **3**, 919 (2000).
9. S. Song and L. F. Abbott, Column and map development and cortical re-mapping through spike-timing dependent plasticity, *Neuron* **32**, 339 (2001).
10. C. Clopath, L. Buesing, E. Vasilaki and W. Gerstner, Connectivity reflects coding: A model of voltage-based spike-timing-dependent-plasticity with homeostasis, *Nature Neuroscience* **13**, 344 (2010).
11. W. Gerstner and W. M. Kistler, *Spiking Neuron Models* (Cambridge University Press, New York, 2002).
12. S. J. Thorpe, D. Fize and C. Marlot, Speed of processing in the human visual system, *Nature* **381**, 520 (1996).
13. J. Rubin, D. D. Lee and H. Sompolinsky, Equilibrium properties of temporally asymmetric Hebbian plasticity, *Physical Review Letters* **86**, 364 (2001), PMID: 11177832.
14. R. Gütig, R. Aharonov, S. Rotter and H. Sompolinsky, Learning input correlations through nonlinear temporally asymmetric Hebbian plas-

ticity, *The Journal of Neuroscience* **23**, 3697 (2003).

15. W. Gerstner, R. Kempter, J. Van Hemmen and H. Wagner, A neuronal learning rule for sub-millisecond temporal coding, *Nature* **383**, 76 (1996).
16. E. M. Izhikevich, J. A. Gally and G. M. Edelman, Spike-timing dynamics of neuronal groups, *Cerebral Cortex* **14**, 933 (2004).
17. V. Braitenberg and A. Schüz, *Cortex: Statistics and Geometry of Neural Connectivity*, 2 edn. (Springer, 1998).
18. T. Wennekers and G. Palm, On the relation between neural modelling and experimental neuroscience, *Theory in Bioscience* **116**, 273 (1997).
19. A. Schüz, D. Chaimow, D. Liewald and M. Dortenman, Quantitative aspects of corticocortical connections: A tracer study in the mouse, *Cerebral Cortex* **16**, 1474 (2006).
20. A. Schüz and V. Braitenberg, The human cortical white matter: Quantitative aspects of cortico-cortical long-range connectivity, in *Cortical Areas: Unity and Diversity*, eds. A. Schüz and R. Miller (Taylor & Francis, London and New York, 2002)
21. E. M. Izhikevich, Polychronization: computation with spikes., *Neural Comput* **18**, 245 (2006).
22. A. Angelucci and P. C. Bressloff, Contribution of feedforward, lateral and feedback connections to the classical receptive field center and extra-classical receptive field surround of primate v1 neurons, *Prog Brain Res* **154**, 93 (2006).

A Critique of Pure Hierarchy: Uncovering Cross-Cutting Structure in a Natural Dataset*

J. L. McClelland
Department of Psychology, Stanford University
Stanford, CA, 94305, USA
E-mail: mcclelland@stanford.edu
www.psych.stanford.edu/~jlm

Z. Sadeghi
School of Electrical and Computer Engineering, University of Tehran,
Tehran, Iran
E-mail: zahra.sadeghi@ut.ac.ir

A. M. Saxe
Center for Brain Science, Harvard University
Cambridge, MA 02138, USA
E-mail: asaxe@stanford.edu
www.stanford.edu/~asaxe

How best can we understand – and visualize – the structure in multi-dimensional data? One common approach is to rely on hierarchical cluster analysis, either for theoretical or for more descriptive reasons. Here, we point out that an apparently revealing hierarchical clustering solution may well be compatible with structure that is not well characterized as a hierarchy. In particular, a hierarchical description can be equally consistent with cross-cutting rather than strictly hierarchical, or nested, structure. We offer an alternative approach, based on inspection of the feature vectors provided by a singular value decomposition (SVD) which allows a flexible mixture of hierarchical and cross-cutting dimensions and which can reveal whether dimensions are cross-cutting or nested. The SVD offers a more flexible representation than a hierarchy in that it can capture either hierarchical or cross-cutting structure or blends of these two structure types, or, indeed, many other structure types. We then introduce a refinement of the SVD approach based on sparse principal component analysis that leads to more easily interpretable dimensions. In our dataset, these dimensions correspond to aquatic vs. land animals, large vs. small animals, predators vs prey animals, and primates vs. other mammals.

Keywords: Semantic knowledge representation; Singular value decomposition; Sparse principal components analysis; Deep neural networks.

* This work is supported in part by a research fellowship from IROST to Z.S. and by fellowship support to A.S. from NSF IGERT Grant 0801700.

1. Background

How do humans represent knowledge of different types of items and their properties? One frequent approach is to assume this knowledge is represented in terms of a hierarchy. In some cases, a hierarchy may be used as a summary presentation of the structure in data, without a strong theoretical commitment. Other times, a hierarchy may be asserted to capture the knowledge that people use in making, for example, similarity judgments or property attributions[1]. In either case, we will suggest, a hierarchical presentation can be misleading if interpreted too literally, and it is at best ambiguous if the limitations of the hierarchical representation are understood. We discuss these issue and propose alternative ways to visualizing structure in data, focusing on a data set that has been used in several studies of the organization of semantic knowledge in the domain of mammals.

Our work draws on a body of prior work culminating with Kemp and Tenenbaum[1], and Glick[2,3]. Kemp and Tenenbaum found that a hierarchical tree structure provided a better fit to human property attribution data from several experiments in the domain of mammals compared to other structures they considered, but the Glick studies found that a hierarchy both failed to fully reflect the similarity structure in the data set and also missed aspects of human similarity and property attribution judgments. The evidence suggests that participants are sensitive to structure that cuts across the branches of the best-fitting taxonomic hierarchy, and is not adequately reflected within it. The focus here is not on an effort to contrast overall theoretical frameworks (Kemp and Tenenbaum's overall framework can be used to capture cross-cutting structure; see Shafto, Kemp, Mansinghka & Tenenbaum[4]), but on the effort to bring broader awareness to the limitations of a hierarchical representation of data. Our approach to overcoming these limitations reflects our interest in exploring ways to characterize structure that may be *quasi-regular,* and thus not fully consistent with *any* specific structure type[5], but the approach is ultimately completely empirical, and can be used to explore the structure in a data set regardless of any prior theoretical commitments.

Neural networks of the kinds we have often used in models are capable of capturing quasi-regular structure, thereby reproducing patterns of human behavior in several quasi-regular domains, such as single word reading and knowledge of objects and their properties. A limitation of the approach, however, is that knowledge in this form is stored in connection weights, and is often hard to intepret[6]. Recently, we have developed a mathematically explicit characterization of the knowledge learned in deep neural networks in terms of a weighted combination of aspects of the structure in a data set as revealed by singular value decomposition[7] (SVD). Our focus here is not on the neural network analysis, but on the SVD itself as a method for representing structure. We show how an SVD can be used to make apparent the underlying cross-cutting or nested structure in a data set that would be lost under a hierarchical clustering analysis, and we discuss an extension of the approach that can further increase the interpretability of the structure it uncovers in natural data.

In what follows, we first consider the data set that will be the focus of our analysis, and point out why no single hierarchy can adequately characterize the knowledge contained within it. Then, we describe how *both* the structure that the hierarchical model captures and the structure that it misses can be captured by a singular value decomposition of the data set. We then note that the singular value decomposition still lacks a degree of interpretability, leading us to explore a variant of the approach based on sparse principal components analysis (SPCA) that produces a more easily interpretable decomposition. The *discussion* section considers the broader implications of our findings for the interpretation of experimental observations and for alternative theoretical frameworks on the nature of human knowledge representations.

2. Dataset and limitations of representing it hierarchically

The data set that will be the focus of our analysis, here called the *50 mammal set*, came originally from Osherson *et al.*[8] and was augmented by Kemp and Tenenbaum[1], who provided it to us. It is worth noting at the outset that this data set is not objective data, but is instead a characterization of human knowledge, so that the effort to discover which sort of representation best characterizes this data set is an exercise in modeling human knowledge, not simply an exercise in modeling facts about objects in the world.

The data set was obtained by asking participants to rate the applicability of each of 85 different predicate terms to each of 50 different mammals, then taking the mean over participants of the ratings in each cell of the 50 animal by 85 property matrix. Figure 1 displays the matrix of correlations of the property vectors of the 50 animals. The items are arranged according to a generic hierarchical clustering solution displayed in Figure 2. That is, items within the same cluster are near each other. If the hierarchy adequately captures all of the structure in the training data, then, similar items should be near each other, and dissimilar items should be farther away. It should be evident from Figure 1 that the hierarchical clustering captures many strong similarity relations (reflected by dark red color near the main diagonal) but also misses many others (dark red colors *not* near the main diagonal). For example, the weasel (21st row or column of the array) is similar to, and grouped with other small mammals (raccoon, rat, weasel, squirrel, etc.), and it shares much in common with them. However, the weasel is almost as similar to the fox and some of the other predators as it is to the small mammals it is grouped with, a fact that is not captured in the hierarchical solution in Figure 2.

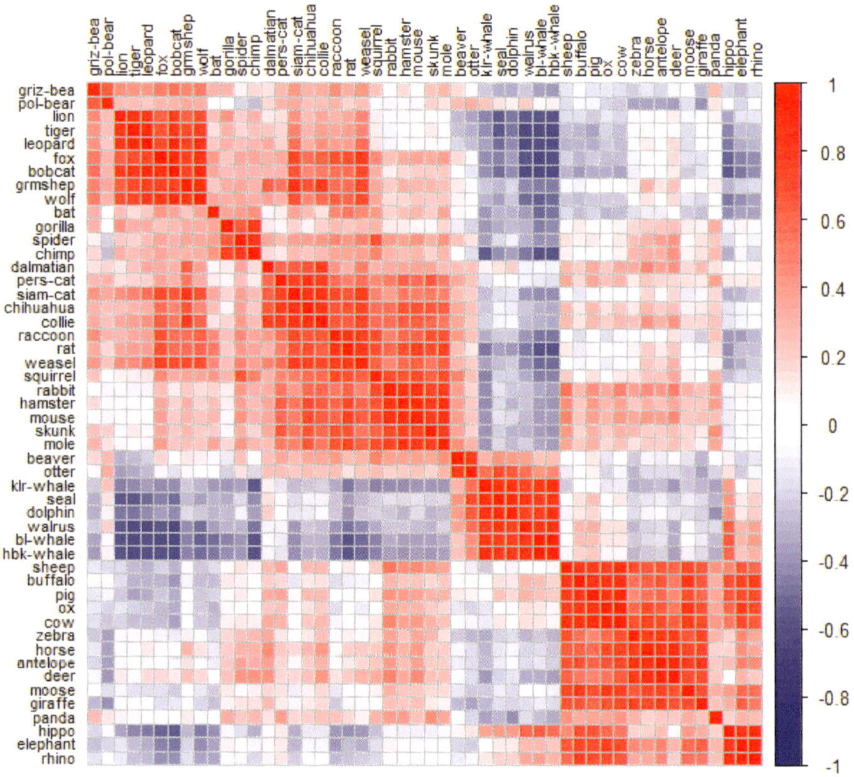

Fig. 1. Correlation matrix for the 50-mammal data set used in Kemp & Tenenbaum[1]. Ordering is based on the hierarchical clustering solution shown in Fig 2.

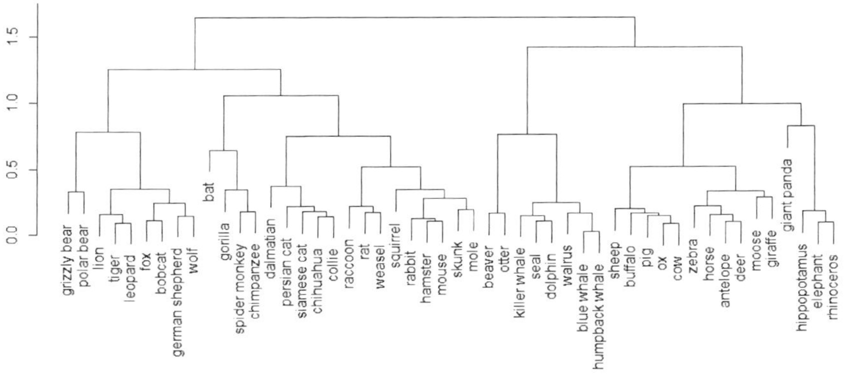

Fig. 2. Hierarchical clustering of the 50 mammal set, obtained with R's **hclust** function. Distances are 1-C, where C is the correlation of the two items' vectors of Manthattan distances to other items.

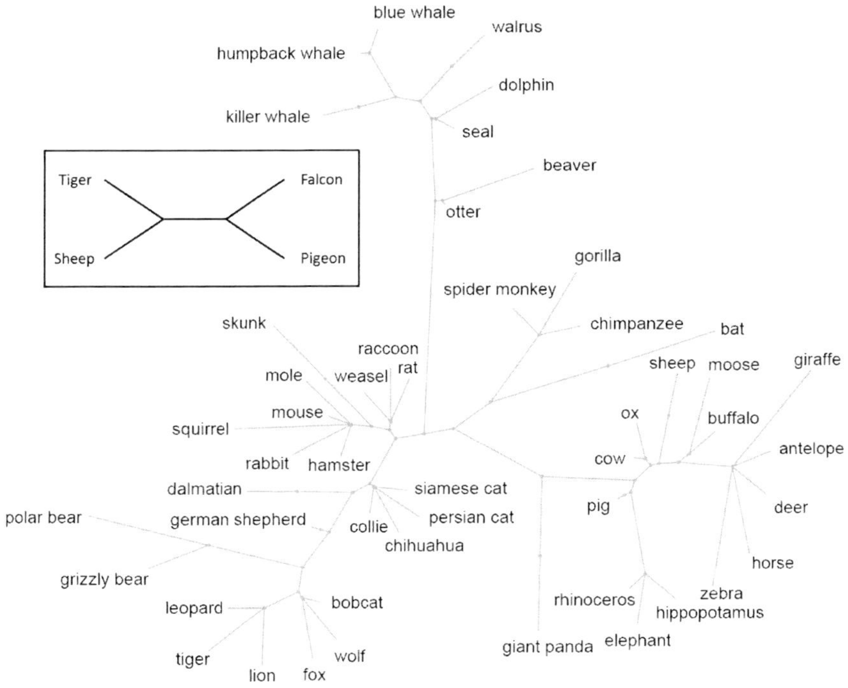

Fig. 3. The best fitting hierarchical diffusion model reported by Kemp and Tenenbaum[1], Fig 3, p. 28, Copyright 2009 American Psychological Association. Reprinted with permission. Inset shows the structure of the minimal hierarchical model that would be fit to both data sets shown in Fig 4. The structure is similar to that in Fig 2, but the bat and primates placed slightly differently.

No single hierarchy can capture the similarity of the weasel to both the small mammals and the predators at the same time, as the weasel can only be placed in one cluster, while (for example) the squirrel and fox belong in these two different clusters. The hierarchical tree is thus a Procrustean bed for this data set, forcing items to fit into a structure that does not suit them well. Figure 3 presents the similar hierarchical solution found by Kemp and Tenenbaum[1]. Their solution is based on a probabilistic property diffusion process, such that properties of items constrain each other by an amount that depends only on the length of the connecting path between items. This length can be directly measured from the graph in Figure 3. It will be seen that their solution has the same difficulty as the more generic hierarchical clustering solution shown in Figure 2. Their model is also a hierarchical model, in that items are connected by a single branching network, such that there is only one path between each pair of animals (there is no privileged root of their tree, but one might imagine one near the center of the figure, where the main vertical branch rises from the main left-right axis). The weasel is again placed close to the other small mammals, forcing the distance to the fox and other predators to be long.

Glick[2,3] pointed to these aspects of the data and went on to show that participants' judgments of the likelihood that a biological property attributed to one animal would also hold of another animal were not fully accounted for by Kemp and Tenenbaum's hierarchical tree. Such judgments were obtained in a property attribution task, which presented a putatively generic premise attributing a fictitious property to a familiar class of objects, such as 'Horses have enzyme X132 in their bloodstream'. Participants then rated the likelihood that other target animals would also have this property. Kemp & Tenenbaum[1] found that their hierarchy provided a better account of previously existing data on such attributions on several subsets of mammals compared to the raw similarities among these items in the 50-mammal dataset. However, Glick used a different subset of animals, including the rat, the fox, and the weasel, and found that participants' ratings did not adhere well to the predictions of the hierarchical model. Glick also obtained similarity judgments between all possible pairs of items in a data set consisting of 50 mammals, 30 birds, and 20 fish. While a hierarchical model with separate branches for mammals, birds, and fish captures the strongest dimensions in this data, it fails to pick up on other factors that are clearly present in the similarity ratings. For example, a mammal and a bird were judged more similar if they were similar in size or ferocity. This similarity cannot be captured in a hierarchical tree, given that all the birds are on one branch of the tree and all of the mammals are on the other. In short a tree has no way of revealing cross-cutting similarity.

To state the limitations of a tree-like structure more formally, only the average value of a property can propagate between sets of items at different ends of a single connecting pathway. In the hierarchy, birds and mammals are on different branches connected by a single pathway (as in the minimal hierarchical model shown in the inset in Figure 3), so that only average values of birds can propagate to mammals and *vice-versa.*

3. An alternative account of semantic structure

As an alternative to a hierarchical approach, we offer the view that semantic structure might best be captured by a more flexible system of representation that can be sensitive to multiple types of structure that may be present in a data set. Our scheme grows out of our past efforts to understand the knowledge learned in deep (i.e., multi-layer) neural networks. Importantly, in our current approach, the knowledge is characterized at a level more abstract than any particular neural network, bringing out the underlying structural relationships present in the data set. The approach relies on the concepts of singular value decomposition (SVD) and the closely related concepts of principal component analysis. Singular value decomposition is also used in the well-known Latent Semantic Analysis approach to semantic representation[9]. We apply it here, not to matrices of word co-occurrences in texts, but to the item-feature matrix, to directly capture the semantic relations among items based on their properties. We focus on an intuitive presentation; for technical details, see Saxe *et al.*[7].

According to our approach, the content of a data set is characterized in terms of a set of underlying dimensions. Each item is placed at a point along each of the dimensions, and each dimension is associated with a vector of features. The placement of an item on a dimension can be considered a classification scheme. For example, for the toy data set in Figure 4 (top) one classification vector would classify items on a bird-mammal dimension (positive end = mammal, negative end = bird). Associated with each classification vector there is a corresponding feature vector. The bird-mammal feature vector assigns high likelihood to *four legs* and *fur* and low likelihood to *wings* and *feathers* for mammals, and the reverse pattern for birds. The total strength of this relationship, expressing how much of the overall variation in the item-property matrix it accounts for, is captured by the strength of the singular value (SV) associated with this dimension (Figure 4, top center).

A virtue of this approach is that it allows for other dimensions either to be hierarchically embedded within the classification captured by a stronger dimension or to cut across such dimensions. In the data set on the top left of Figure 4, we see that there are two predators and two pray animals, and in each

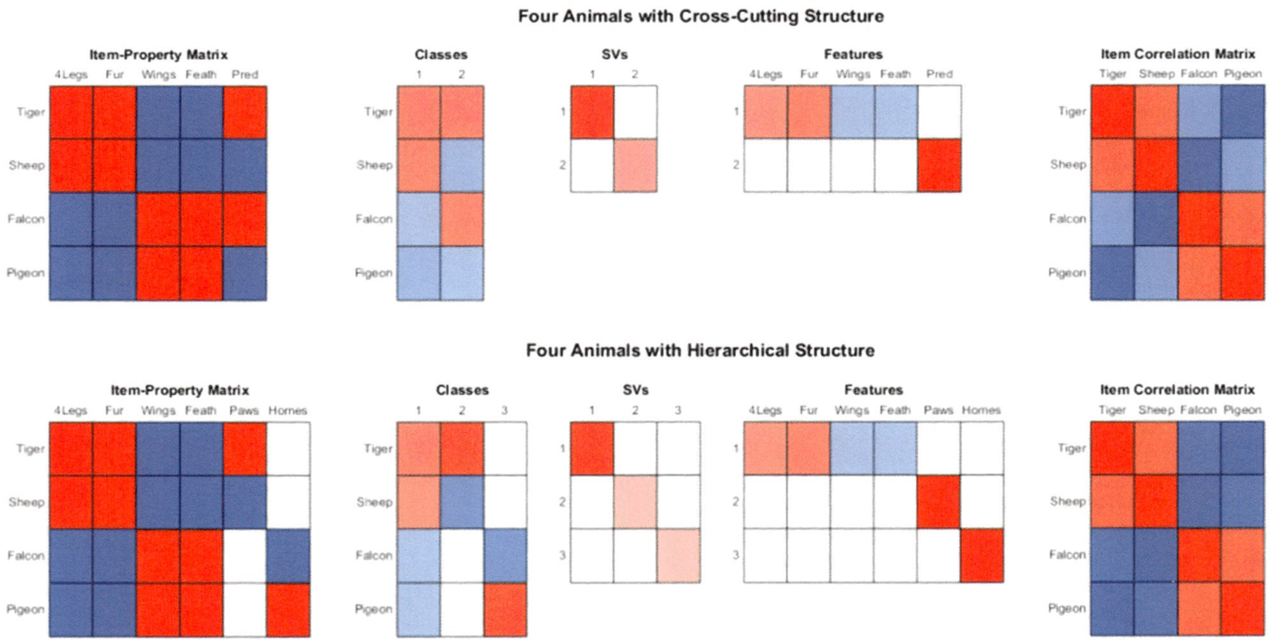

Fig. 4. A data set with cross-cutting structure (top row) and another with hierarchical structure (bottom row). Left panels are the data sets themselves. Singular value decomposition (middle panels) brings out the differences in the structure, revealing a second cross-cutting dimension in the first case and two embedded dimensions in the second case. These different structures are associated with distinct correlation matrices (right panels) revealing cross-cutting structure in the top row but not in the bottom row. A hierarchical model like that of Kemp and Tenenbaum cannot capture these cross-cutting similarities in the data set shown in the top row, and would produce a correlation matrix like the one associated with the truly hierarchical data set in both cases.

case one is a mammal and the other is a bird. Thus predator status is a cross-cutting dimension. It can be represented as a single additional classification dimension (positive for predators, negative for prey) and a corresponding feature vector. In this simplified example, there is a single *predator* feature, but the scheme will accommodate sets of features such as *has sharp claws, eats animals*, etc., that tend to occur in predators but not in non-predators.

Alternatively, additional dimensions can be embedded within each of the higher-level dimensions, as represented in the alternative data set shown in the second row of Figure 4. In this case, one feature distinguishes among the two mammals (e.g., *has paws*), while the other distinguishes between the two birds (*flies home* or *homes*). What is critical here is that additional dimensions can either be cross-cutting or they can be further sub-categorizing dimensions. In the latter case, they show up in the SVD as two separate dimensions, each with its own classification and feature-specification vector. Thus, the SVD is capable of distinguishing these two types of structure. However, a hierarchical clustering analysis will necessarily treat both kinds of dimensions the same, failing to distinguish the two types of structure. Specifically, the two different SVDs each fully capture the structure present in the corresponding data set, as illustrated by the correlation matrices reconstructed from each SVD on the right of each row of the figure. In contrast, the hierarchical tree for both data sets has the structure shown in the inset to Figure 3 with a corresponding correlation matrix like that appropriate for a data set where the structure is truly hierarchical, as in the second row of Figure 4.

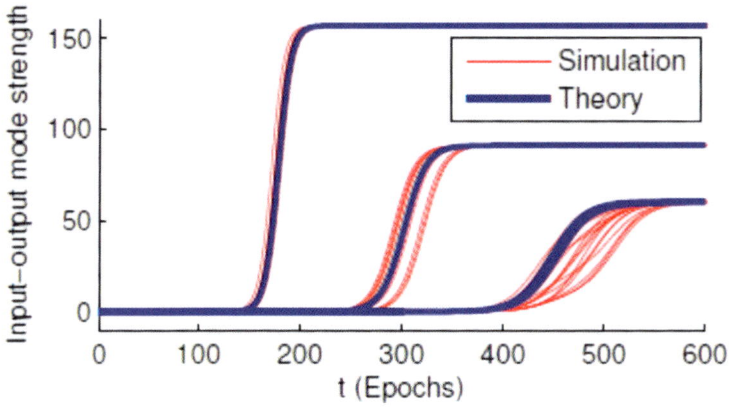

Fig. 5. Time course of learning in a linear network trained with a set of item-feature pairs characterized by three singular dimensions, each with different strengths. From Figure 3, p. 1274 of Saxe, McClelland and Ganguli[7]. Copyright 2013, the authors. Reprinted with permission.

In addition to its use in flexibly capturing these and other types of structure which can be mixed within the same data set, the SVD approach can also be linked to the gradual learning process that occurs in a deep neural network. Rogers and McClelland[10] studied this process as it arises in the semantic network model introduced by Rumelhart and Todd[11]. A subsequent mathematical analysis by Saxe, McClelland and Ganguli[7] demonstrated that the learning dynamics exhibited by such networks can be well-captured with a simplified (i.e., linearized) version of the same deep network. Space prevents a detailed review here; suffice it to say that the time course of learning in both the original, non-linear network and the simplified linear version of the network, when trained on a given set of training examples, is well captured by the statement that the learned connection weights learn the singular dimensions that characterize the data set in a stage-like fashion, as shown in Figure 5. Quantitatively, the strength of the representation of each singular dimension increasing with time according to a highly *non-linear* function:

$$s(t) = (Se^{2St/\tau})/(e^{2St/\tau} - 1 + S/s_0)$$

where $s(t)$ represents the strength of the dimension after time t, S represents the strength of the underlying singular value, s_0 represents the initial strength of the dimension (which will have a small random value in a randomly initialized neural network), and τ is a time constant depending on the network's learning rate. According to this function, shown for a training set characterized by three singular values in Figure 5, each singular dimension is acquired after a time that depends on the size of its singular value. This kind of pattern is similar to the stage-like progression seen in many developmental transitions[12] and in non-linear neural networks like those applied to development by Rogers and McClelland[10] or McClelland[13].

4. Uncovering the structure in the 50-mammal data set

A difficulty with singular value decomposition when applied to a natural data set (such as the 50-mammal data set) is that the resulting dimensions are not necessarily easily interpretable. While these dimensions may be the true dimensions that characterize the structure in the data and are the ones the deep network successively extracts, they do not necessarily correspond to easily interpretable aspects of the underlying data. We do not find this problematic, since we expect natural structure to be *quasi-regular,* rather than truly systematic[14,15]. We can still ask, though, how cognitively interpretable dimensions might arise from experience with a set of items. One possibility is that such dimensions are constrained to account for strong patterns of co-variation present in a body of experiences while relying only on a small number of features. The motivation for this might either be cognitive economy or simplicity in describing these dimensions to others. To explore this possibility, we explored the dimensions discovered by sparse principal component analysis[16] (SPCA). Our explorations employed a variant of SPCA that extracts components sequentially (**spca** function from the SpaSM toolbox[17]).

First we note how standard principal component analysis (PCA) relates to the SVD approach we have described thus far. A standard PCA when applied to a data set such as ours returns a set of *coefficient vectors* that each correspond to the *feature vectors* returned by the SVD of the same data set, as well as a set of *score* that play the role of the *classification vectors* in the SVD, but with each score vector equal to the corresponding classification vector of the SVD scaled by the corresponding singular value. Each successive coefficient vector is chosen to be orthogonal to all previous co-efficient vectors and to maximize the amount of residual or remaining variance it explains.

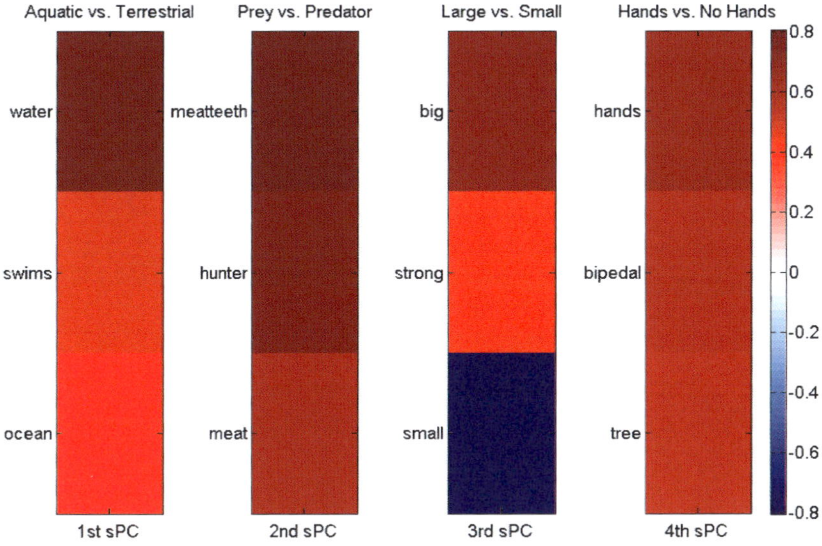

Fig. 6. Feature loadings on the first four sparse coefficient vectors found by the **spca** function (K >= 4, delta = 5, stop = -3) of Sjöstrand *et al.*[17].

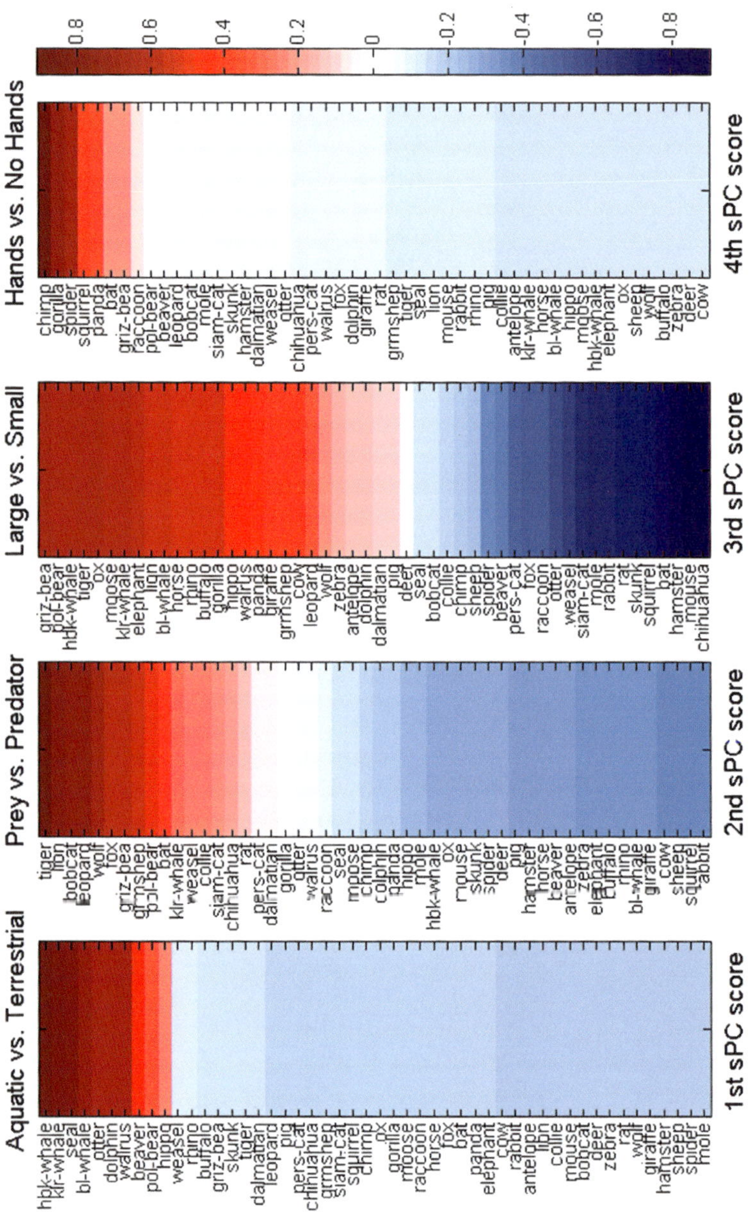

Fig. 7. Item scores on the first four sparse principal components.

The sequential SPCA algorithm we have used is like PCA in maximizing variance explained by each successive coefficient vector and in choosing orthogonal directions, but the selection of vectors is constrained so that the coefficient vectors are sparse.[†] We experimented with different sparsities (number of non-zero coefficients) and found that the clearest results were obtained using a sparsity of 3. The first four resulting feature and score vectors are shown in Figures 6 & 7. The first dimension identifies aquatic vs. non-aquatic mammals; the second identifies predators vs. prey; and the third picks out the size dimension. It is important to note that these are *cross-cutting* dimensions. The whales are all highly aquatic, but whereas the killer whale lies at one end of the predator/prey dimension, the blue whale lies near the other end. Similarly, though the seal is highly aquatic, it is well separated from the whales in size.

The fourth dimension is also interpretable, and can be thought of in different ways. We have named this dimension after its most highly-weighted feature, hands, short for 'has hands'. The dimension also has large weights for 'bipedal' and 'tree', short for 'is bipedal', and 'lives in trees'. This cluster of features most strongly picks out the primates in the data set -- the chimp, the gorilla, and the spider monkey (note that size cuts across this dimension, since the three primates are of very different sizes). However, primarily because of the association (in the responses of the human participants who made the property attribution ratings) of all three types of primates with trees, the tree feature is included in the cluster, with the consequence that other, non-primate species that are also associated with trees score reasonably high on this dimension. This illustrates that the dimensions are ultimately defined by correlations and cannot be seen as necessarily separating characteristic from defining features or as selecting features of a homogeneous type. Dimensions of this kind might influence implicit or intuitive cognitive judgments, even if they do not necessarily capture the kinds of dimensions a scientist might use to organize information about the properties of objects[18].

The SPCs capture information also captured in Kemp and Tenenbaum's hierarchical analysis, as well as information not captured there. In particular, the aquatic dimension picked out by the SPCA is essentially the same dimension as the one captured along the vertical axis of Kemp and Tenenbaum's tree (see

---

[†] It should be noted that imposing a sparsity constraint of the feature vectors used in a PCA is not the same as imposing a sparsity constraint on the number of active units in a distributed representation of a given input[21]. The words *sparse* and *sparsity* are used in both contexts but the entities these terms describe are different in the two cases and it is useful to realize that there is a distinction between these usages.

Figure 3). The 'hands' dimension is associated with the small cluster of primates also found in Kemp and Tenenbaum's tree. However, the prey-predator and size dimensions are not well captured in the tree. The tree picks out a set of large non-predators (lower right), but there are large and small prey and predator animals sprinkled throughout the top and bottom-left branches, as well as size variations within many branches.

In a further analysis, we found that each of the first few dimensions the SPCA discovers is more similar to the corresponding standard, non-sparse PC than to any of the other standard PCs, although the sparse PCs do have some cross-similarity with several non-sparse PCs. This finding is shown in Figure 8, which shows the projection of each of the first 5 sparse PCs onto each of the first five non-sparse PCs. We see the strongest positive values along the diagonal, but we also find non-zero off-diagonal projections. As examples, the first sparse PC projects most strongly onto the first standard PC but also has a fairly strong negative projection onto the second standard PC, while the second sparse PC has moderately strong positive projections onto the first and third standard PCs. Looking at these results in another way, we can say that the first standard PC has non-negligible projections onto all of the first 5 sparse PCs, indicating that the first standard PC reflects a mixture of the interpretable dimensions identified by the sparse principal component analysis.

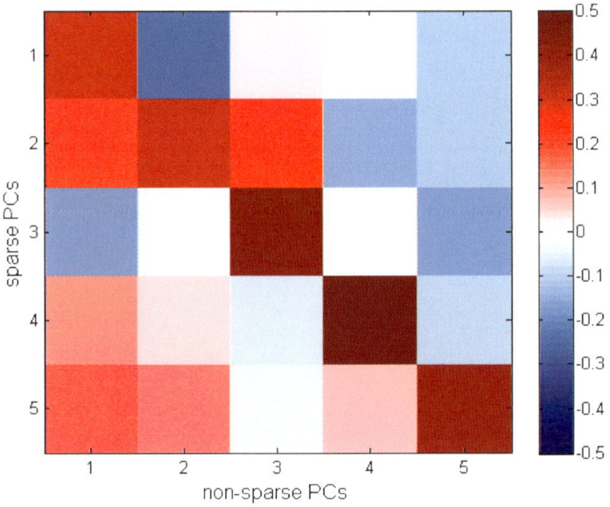

Fig. 8. Projections of the first five sparse principal components onto the first five non-sparse principal components of the 50 mammal data set.

5. Discussion

Our results highlight the fact that a tree structure may often provide an imperfect guide to the full structure present in a data set. In particular, a hierarchical tree is bound to hide semantic distinctions that cut across levels of the tree. While Kemp & Tenenbaum found some support for the view that human subjects, like their hierarchy, discard this cross-cutting information when making property attribution judgments, Glick[2] probed this matter further, and showed that such cross-cutting information does influence attribution judgments as well as item similarity judgments. These points led us to argue for models capable of representing blended, hybrid structural forms that can include both hierarchical as well as cross-cutting structure. In other work[19], we have also found that the more flexible approach to structure characterization offered by singular value decomposition and principal component analysis may help reveal cross-category associations that further contribute to semantic knowledge about items, beyond the properties of the items themselves.

Flexible structure is naturally captured by deep neural network models, but the dimensions these models find are not necessarily easily interpretable. We are not discomforted by the possibility that natural structure is not perfectly characterizable in terms that are easily interpretable, and we stress that these dimensions might still underlie human similarity and property attribution judgments, even if they are difficult to fully describe in words; further research on this topic will certainly be warranted.

In the meantime, the present work has focused on finding a way of projecting the knowledge that is captured in a deep neural network onto dimensions that may be more easily described. Our investigations indicate that such projections can be provided by including a sparsity constraint limiting the number of features used in each representational dimension. These dimensions bear some similarity to the corresponding non-sparse dimensions, but are more easily interpretable, and may be useful as a projection of the real knowledge underlying intuitive semantic judgments into dimensions that can be described in words. These dimensions are, however, still fundamentally derived from purely statistical considerations, and can combine information of very different types (as in the case of the fourth dimension, which combines 'has hands' and 'lives in trees', properties that happen to correlate in the ratings for the primates in the data set).

Implications for modeling frameworks. We would like to stress that our critique of a pure hierarchy as a representation of semantic knowledge is not intended as a critique of any particular approach to understanding human knowledge representation. The points made here and in the work of Glick[2] are criticisms of hierarchical models, whether they come from the tradition of structured probabilistic models, as the model of Kemp and Tenenbaum does, or from more generic hierarchical data analysis methods, as shown in Figure 2. Hierarchical models of whatever provenance obscure cross-cutting structure, and such structure plays a role in the similarity judgments and property attributions of human subjects. As noted earlier, Kemp, Tenenbaum, and colleagues have discussed ways of capturing combinations of structure types[20,4]. A structured probabilistic model of human semantic knowledge different from the one they presented in their 2009 paper could potentially address most of our concerns.

We would note, however, that it may be possible to represent and be sensitive to structure without relying on *any* explicit structural form[5]. A singular valued decomposition or deep neural network can, as we have seen, capture either hierarchical or cross-cutting structure or a blend of hierarchical and cross-cutting structure *without explicitly entertaining either structure type.* Indeed, the range of structure types that can be captured in this approach includes many other structure types, as well as arbitrary blends of such structure types, and even data sets that do not strictly conform to, but only approximate, such structure types. Thus, any explicit specification of a particular structure type can be misleading unless it is understood as a descriptive approximation rather than an actual characterization of the representation underlying human semantic cognition.

References

1. Kemp, C., & Tenenbaum, J. B. (2009). Structured statistical models of inductive reasoning. *Psychological Review*, **116,** 1, 20–58.
2. Glick, J. J. (2011). *Uncovering the organization of semantic structure with similarity and inductions.* Doctoral dissertation, Psychology department, Stanford University.
3. Glick, J. J., & McClelland, J. L. (2010). Semantics in the wild: Context-sensitive inferences about mammals. In S. Ohlsson & R. Catrambone (Eds.), *Proceedings of the 32nd Annual Conference of the Cognitive Science Society* (p.668). Austin, TX: Cognitive Science Society.
4. Shafto, P., Kemp, C., Mansinghka, V., & Tenenbaum, J. B. (2011). A probabilistic model of cross-categorization. *Cognition*, **120**, 1, 1–25.
5. McClelland, J. L., Botvinick, M. M., Noelle, D. C., Plaut, D. C., Rogers, T.T., Seidenberg, M. S., & Smith, L. B. (2010). Letting Structure Emerge: Connectionist and Dynamical Systems Approaches to Understanding Cognition. *Trends in Cognitive Sciences*, **14**, 348–356.

6. McCloskey, M. (1991). Networks and theories: The place of connectionism in cognitive science. *Psychological Science*, **2,** 6, 387-395.
7. Saxe, A. M., McClelland, J. L., & Ganguli, S. (2013). Learning hierarchical category structure in deep neural networks. In M. Knauff, M. Paulen, N. Sebanz, & I. Wachsmuth (Eds.), *Proceedings of the 35th annual meeting of the Cognitive Science Society*. (pp. 1271-1276). Austin, TX: Cognitive Science Society.
8. Osherson, D. N., Stern, J., Wilkie, O., Stob, M., & Smith, E. E. (1991). Default probability. *Cognitive Science*, **15**, 251–269.
9. Landauer, T. K., & Dumais, S. T. (1997). A solution to Plato's problem: The latent semantic analysis theory of acquisition, induction, and representation of knowledge. *Psychological review*, **104**, 2, 211.
10. Rogers, T. T. & McClelland, J. L. (2004). *Semantic Cognition: A Parallel Distributed Processing Approach.* Cambridge, MA: MIT Press.
11. Rumelhart, D. E., & Todd, P. M. (1993). Learning and connectionist representations. In D. E. Meyer & S. Kornblum (Eds.), *Attention and Performance XIV: Synergies in Experimental Psychology, Artificial Intelligence, and Cognitive Neuroscience* (pp. 3-30). Cambridge, MA: MIT Press.
12. McClelland, J. L. (1994). The interaction of nature and nurture in development: A parallel distributed processing perspective. In P. Bertelson, P. Eelen, & G. d'Ydewalle (Eds.), *International Perspectives on Psychological Science, Volume 1: Leading Themes.* United Kingdom: Erlbaum.
13. McClelland, J. L. (1989). Parallel distributed processing: Implications for cognition and development. In Morris, R. (Ed)., *Parallel distributed processing: Implications for psychology and neurobiology.* (pp. 8-45). New York: Oxford University Press.
14. Seidenberg, M. S., & McClelland, J. L. (1989). A distributed, developmental model of word recognition and naming. *Psychological review*, **96**, 4, 523-568.
15. McClelland, J. L. (2015). Capturing gradience, continuous change, and quasi-regularity in sound, word, phrase, and meaning. In B. MacWhinney & W. O'Grady (Eds.), *The Handbook of Language Emergence*, Chaper 2, pp. 54-80. Hoboken, NJ: John Wiley & Sons.
16. Zou, H., Hastie, T. & Tibshirani, R. (2006) Sparse Principal Component Analysis. *Journal of Computational and Graphical Statistics*, **15**, 2, 265-286.

17. Sjöstrand, K., Clemmensen, L. H., Larsen, R., & Ersbøll, B. (2012). Spasm: A matlab toolbox for sparse statistical modeling. *Journal of Statistical Software*, *VV* (Issue I).
18. Goldberg, R. F., & Thompson-Schill, S. L. (2009). Developmental "roots" in mature biological knowledge. *Psychological Science*, **20**, 4, 480-487.
19. Sadeghi, Z., McClelland, J. L., & Hoffman, P. (2015). You shall know an object by the company it keeps: An investigation of semantic representations derived from object co-occurrence in visual scenes. *Neuropsychologia*, **76**, 52-61.
20. Kemp, C., & Tenenbaum, J. B. (2008). The discovery of structural form. *PNAS*, **105**, 31, 10687-10692.
21. Olshausen, B. A. (1996). Emergence of simple-cell receptive field properties by learning a sparse code for natural images. *Nature*, **381**, 6583, 607-609.

Implementing the "Simple" Model of Reading Deficits: A Connectionist Investigation of Interactivity

Padraic Monaghan
Department of Psychology, Lancaster University, Lancaster, UK
E-mail: p.monaghan@lancaster.ac.uk

Anna M. Woollams
School of Psychological Sciences, University of Manchester, Manchester, UK

The "Simple model" of reading proposes that reading deficits can be understood in terms of single or combined contributions of comprehension and phonological impairments[1]. Phonological or semantic deficits have been effectively tested in isolation in computational models of reading, and their results map onto the predictions of the simple model. However, the subtle interactions between impaired representations have not yet been fully explored. We implemented a connectionist triangle model of reading which learned to map between orthographic, phonological, and semantic representations of words for a large sample of monosyllabic words in English. During learning, the model was impaired in terms of its ability to stably represent phonological or semantic information. The model was then tested on a variety of word and picture naming tasks. The model replicated previous studies of dyslexia resulting from a phonological deficit, and comprehension difficulties resulting from a semantic deficit. However, we also found that impairment at either phonological or semantic representations affected the fidelity of representations throughout the model, indicating that pure deficits in reading will be difficult to observe. The implemented model provides constraints on the extent to which phonological and semantic information may interact in order to explain reading and its deficits.

Keywords: Reading; Connectionist modelling; Triangle model; Simple model; Dyslexia; Comprehension deficit; Specific language impairment.

1. Theoretical and implemented models of reading

Learning to read involves acquiring mappings from orthographic forms of words onto phonological forms, to enable naming, and onto semantic forms to ensure that the word is comprehended. There are alternate approaches for how reading disorders are conceived within this abstract characterisation of reading. One view is that reading disorders are categorical. Such an approach gives rise to a taxonomy of reading disorders which affect either phonological processing, semantic processing, or a combination with distinct aetiologies and independent patterns of deficits. Hence, a reading impairment such as dyslexia is conceived as a type of disorder to be described and to be understood independently from a comprehension deficit, or from specific language impairment, or from normative reading performance.

An alternative viewpoint is that deficits can be better conceived as combinations of impairments to a smaller set of dimensions, that are also continuous with unimpaired reading performance. Such alternative accounts of categorical versus dimensional approaches are present in other domains of psychological functioning, such as characterizing personality disorders[2], and though they represent different traditions they have profound implications for understanding of disorders as unitary or multi-componential, comprising either independent or related sets of deficits. A highly influential theoretical model taking this dimensional perspective is the "Simple" model of reading[1,3], which contends that a broad set of reading disorders can be conceived of in terms of ranges of ability along a phonological processing and a semantic processing dimension. The model is shown in Figure 1. Under this view, there are inter-relations between different types of reading disorder. Dyslexia is conceived of as an impairment to the phonological processing dimension, but with intact semantic processing. Poor comprehension is seen as an impairment only to the semantic processing dimension, and specific language impairment is described as indicating an impairment to both phonological and semantic processing. There may then be shared contributions to the origin of the impairment, and consequently overlap in the therapeutic interventions best applied to each "type" of impairment.

Over the last 25 years, computational models have made great headway in implementing alternative theories of reading disorders, and demonstrating the cognitive processing deficits that can give rise to patterns of behavior associated with different deficits[4]. Implementing a computational model of reading enables a test of the adequacy of a theory and the means to decide between alternative theoretical accounts. Previous computational models of reading development have tended to address only a single reading disorder, and to our knowledge there are no systematic attempts to implement and test the Simple model of developmental reading disorders in a single framework. We first review computational models of reading that have simulated either phonological or semantic processing deficits, before presenting our own implemented version of the Simple model. We test the extent to which disorders in distinct dimensions can be independent or whether they are interactive, and the implications of this for theories of dyslexia, poor comprehension, and specific language impairment. We employ the connectionist triangle model in this paper because it has been related to the simple model of developmental reading disorders[1]. Connectionist models are ideal for application to developmental disorders because the requirement to learn the task of mapping between representations enables us to determine the role of disruptions during development, rather than impairing a static, intact model which necessarily requires implementation of assumptions about the dynamics of the system reacting to the deficit (e.g., [5]).

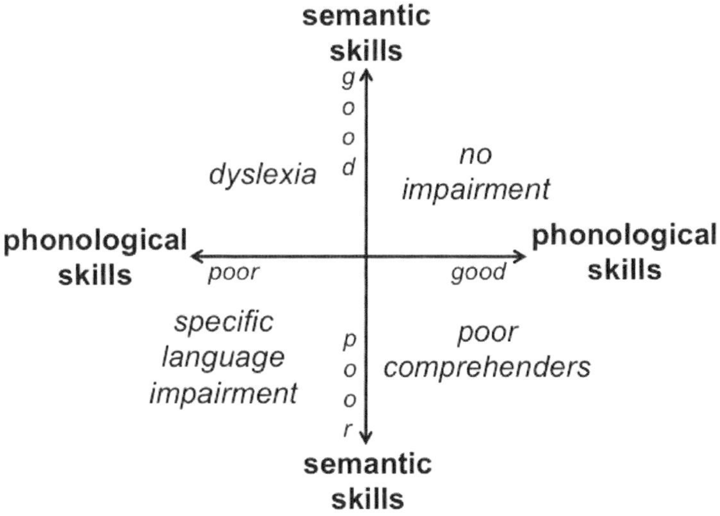

Fig. 1. The Simple model of reading, adapted from [1].

2. Computational models of phonological and semantic reading deficits

The triangle model is one conception of the way in which different types of representation of a word can be learned and interact during learning and processing. The model is shown in Figure 2. Connections between orthographic, phonological, and semantic representations provide the model with the facility to pass activation between representations. A key design feature of this model is its interactivity[6]. Thus, for mapping from orthography to phonology, simulating a reading aloud task, the model permits activation directly from orthography to phonology, but also indirectly via semantics.

Within the triangle modeling framework, there have been several successful attempts to simulate developmental reading disorders. Harm and Seidenberg[7] tested the phonological processing deficit theory of dyslexia by constructing a connectionist model that learned to map from orthography to phonology, with phonological attractors assisting the model in generating stable phonological representations for words. The model was thus a subset of the triangle model, omitting semantics. A phonological deficit was simulated by adding noise to the attractor units, thereby preventing the model from generating efficient phonological representations. The model without impairment learned to read all words in the vocabulary, and was also able to effectively generalize to nonwords. The impaired model, however, demonstrated particular difficulties in reading nonwords, a characteristic of phonological dyslexia.

A fragment of the triangle model has also been used to simulate specific language impairment in terms of a severe phonological deficit. Joanisse and Seidenberg[8] and Joanisse[9] constructed models that learned to map from phonology to semantics. The model was implemented with a phonological processing deficit by adding noise to the input phonological representations. The model was shown to have particular difficulties in processing inflectional morphology (e.g., generating the –ed ending for verbs to indicate past tense)[10] and in accurately determining anaphoric resolution (e.g., linking *him* with *John* in *John says Mary likes him*), both characteristics of specific language impairment.

These subsets of the triangle model, therefore, are effective in simulating a range of behaviors, however, training and testing the full triangle model may result in a rather different perspective than that gained from these simulations of isolated disorders within just a part of the whole model. This is because of the proposed interactivity of the full triangle model. Harm and Seidenberg[11] demonstrated in the fully implemented triangle model that there was division of labor during reading via the direct and indirect pathways for both reading aloud (orthography to phonology mappings) and reading comprehension (orthography to semantics) tasks. This interactivity can then contribute not only to indirect activation passing round an unimpaired model but also to propagation of a deficit within one representation affecting mappings between other representations that are not directly implicated in the task at hand.

3. Architecture

The model is shown in Figure 2. It is derived from the connectionist triangle model of Harm and Seidenberg[11], which comprises a set of phonological units, where spoken word forms are represented, which are connected to and from a set of semantic units, where the meaning of a word is represented. Both the phonological and semantic units are self-connected to a set of attractor units, which enable stable phonological and semantic representations of words to be maintained. There were 200 units in the phonology layer, 2446 units in the semantics layer, 500 units in each of the layers interconnecting the phonology and semantics layers, and 50 units each in the attractor layers.

The orthography of a word was represented across 364 units of the orthography layer, which was connected to the phonological and semantic layers respectively via hidden layers each containing 500 units.

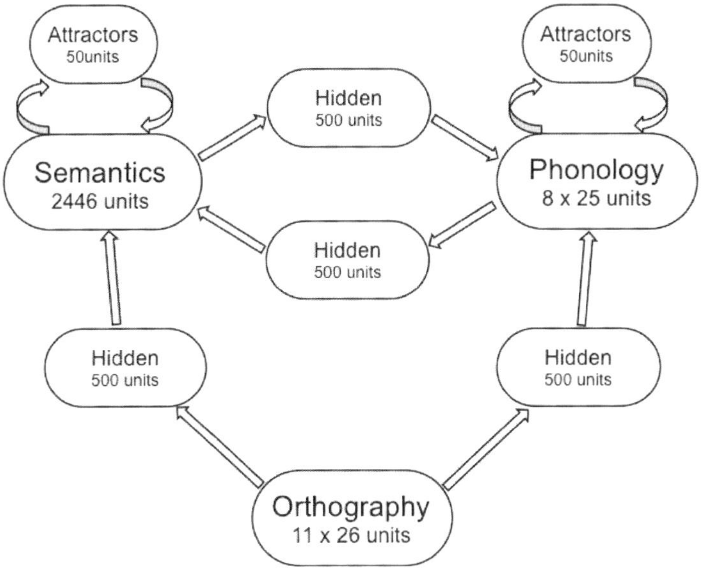

Fig. 2. The triangle model of reading, implementing the simple model of reading impairments. Arrows in the diagram indicate full connectivity between layers in the model.

4. Training and testing

4.1. *Representations*

The model was trained on 6229 monosyllabic words in English. Phonological representations were derived from CELEX[12], with words represented as a sequence of 8 phoneme slots (up to 3 for onset, 1 for vowel, and up to 4 for the coda), with each phoneme represented in terms of 25 phonological feature units. Semantic representations were those used by [11], which were generated from Wordnet[13], and comprised 2446 semantic feature units. A word's semantic representation activated a subset of these semantic features, such that words with similar meaning were represented in terms of an overlapping set of features.

Orthographic representations were represented in terms of 11 letter slots (up to 4 slots for letters corresponding to the word's onset, 2 for the vowel, and up to 5 for letters corresponding to the word's coda) each comprising 26 units, with one unit active for each letter of the alphabet. The word was positioned such that the first vowel of the word appeared in the central letter slot in the orthographic input. Activation of all units in the model was between 0 and 1.

4.2. *Impairing processing in the model*

A model without impairment was compared to models with impairment to either the phonological processing or the semantic processing within the model. Impairment was simulated by adding Gaussian noise with mean 0 and variance 0.5 to the activations of units in either the phonological layer or the semantic layer. This was intended to simulate difficulties in forming stable and accurate representations for words in terms of phonological or semantic processing. The impairment was applied throughout training, as processing deficits precede the onset of reading, and an impairment that is developmental can result in a very different configuration of a cognitive system that adapts to the deficit compared to a system that undergoes an impairment after learning a skill [14].

4.3. *Pretraining*

The model was initially trained to learn to map between the phonological and semantic layers. This was to simulate the child's exposure to spoken language before commencing to learn to read. The model was trained to map from phonological to semantic representations (to simulate spoken word comprehension), or from semantic to phonological representations (to simulate spoken word production). 40% of learning trials were word comprehension and 40% were word production tasks, and there were also 10% of trials each where the model learned to maintain a stable representation of phonology (where the model was presented with a phonological representation and was required to reproduce this over a series of time steps), or of semantics (where a semantic input was maintained until the end of the time steps).

For each trial there were 12 time steps, with the input representation being presented to the model at time step 1, and error was computed based on the model's performance at time step 12. Words were selected randomly according to their log-compressed frequency (see [11] for details), and there were 700,000 training trials. The model learned with backpropagation through time, and the learning rate was 0.02 for the first 500,000 trials, then reduced to 0.01 for the remaining 200,000 trials.

4.4. *Learning to read*

After the model had been pre-trained on mapping between phonology and semantics, the model was then trained to map from orthography to phonology and semantics. For these reading trials, at time step 1, the orthographic input was presented to the model, then from time step 6 to 12, the model was required to produce the phonological and semantic representations for the word. The model was trained using backpropagation through time with learning rate 0.2. As we were interested in early stages of reading development, we stopped training after 400,000 trials before the model had reached 100% performance on forming the mappings. Performance of the models with no impairment, with phonological impairment, and with semantic impairment were compared for reading comprehension (orthography to semantics) and reading aloud (orthography to phonology) tasks.

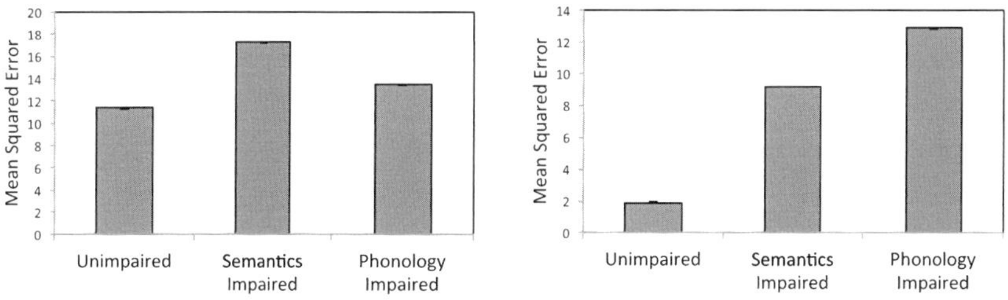

Fig. 3. Performance of the unimpaired, phonological impaired, and semantic impaired models for a spoken word comprehension task (left) and a speech production task (right). Error bars in all Figures show ±1 SEM.

5. Results

5.1. *Pretraining performance*

The models with different patterns of impairment were compared on their performance on spoken word comprehension (phonological input mapping to semantic output) and on spoken word production (semantics input mapping to phonological output). The models' ability to process these tasks was assessed by determining the mean squared error, which was the square of the difference between the target representation for each word, and the models' actual production. The results for each of these tasks are shown in Figure 3.

For the spoken word comprehension task, the unimpaired model resulted in lower error than the semantic impaired model, $t(6228) = 121.334$, $p < .001$, $d = 3.075$. Also, as predicted, the phonological impaired model resulted in lower error than the semantic impaired model, $t(6228) = 92.597$, $p < .001$, $d = 2.346$. However, the unimpaired model also had lower error than the phonological impaired model, $t(6228) = 44.119$, $p < .001$, $d = 1.118$.

For the spoken word production task, as predicted the unimpaired model resulted in lower error than the phonological impaired model, $t(6228) = 192.159$, $p < .001$, $d = 4.869$. However, the semantic impaired model also resulted in greater impairment for this task than no impairment, $t(6228) = 145.784$, $p < .001$, $d = 3.694$. The phonological impaired model resulted in greater error than the semantic impaired model, $t(6228) = 91.478$, $p < .001$, $d = 2.318$.

Hence, affecting the fidelity of the output representation for these tasks resulted in the greatest increase in error, but processing difficulties for the input for either task also increased error compared to an unimpaired model.

Next, we investigated the effect of impairment on the model's ability to recognize and represent different inflectional morphemes, similar to the analyses of [9]. For the word comprehension task, we investigated the activation of the particular semantic unit corresponding to the meaning of morphemes which commonly cause difficulty in specific language impairment: the plural –s marker ending a noun, the third-person -s marker ending a verb, and the past-tense –ed marker ending a verb. Each of these was represented by an individual feature unit in the semantic representation for the word. There were 1515 words with the noun –s, 250 words with the verb –s, and 331 verbs with –ed in the dataset. The error for the model in producing just the semantic feature associated with the meaning of the inflectional morpheme, rather than the error over the whole word, was calculated. The results are shown in Figure 4.

An ANOVA with morpheme type (noun –s, verb –s, verb –ed) as between-item factor, and impairment (none, semantic, phonological) as within-item factor was conducted on mean squared error for the semantic features. There was a significant main effect of morpheme type, $F(2, 2093) = 338.086$, $p < .001$, $\eta_p^2 = .244$, with highest error for the –ed morpheme, then the verb –s, then the noun –s morphemes, all differences $p < .001$. There was also a main effect of impairment type, $F(2, 4186) = 3415.242$, $p < .001$, $\eta_p^2 = .620$, with semantic impairment resulting in most error, followed by phonological impairment, then no impairment, all differences $p < .001$. The interaction between morpheme type and impairment was also significant, $F(4, 4186) = 188.853$, $p < .001$, $\eta_p^2 = .153$, with the greatest difference in error across the models with different impairments for the noun –s morpheme and the smallest difference for the verb –ed morpheme.

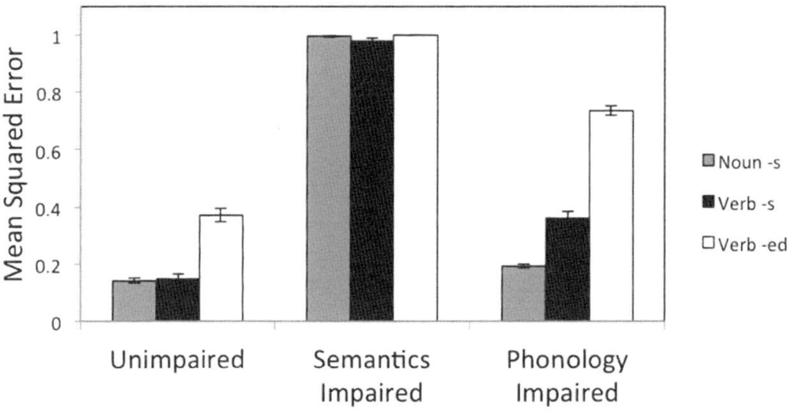

Fig. 4. Performance of the unimpaired, phonological impaired, and semantic impaired models for a reproduction of inflectional morphemes in a word comprehension task.

5.2. *Reading performance*

The models' performance on a reading aloud task was assessed by measuring the mean squared error of the phonological output of the model given an orthographic input. For reading comprehension task, the mean squared error of the semantic output of the model was investigated. The results for the two tasks are shown in Figure 5. For the reading comprehension measure, no impairment resulted in lower error than both semantic impairment, $t(6228) = 52.946$, $p < .001$, $d = 1.342$, and than the phonological impairment, $t(6228) = 45.418$, $p < .001$, $d = 1.151$. The phonological impairment resulted in lower error than the semantic impairment, $t(6228) = 11.051$, $p < .001$, $d = 0.28$.

For the reading aloud task, no impairment resulted in lower error than a phonological impairment, $t(6228) = 116.161$, $p < .001$, $d = 2.944$, and also a lower error than a semantic impairment, $t(6228) = 110.035$, $p < .001$, $d = 2.788$. The semantic impairment resulted in lower error than the phonological impairment, $t(6228) = 17.893$, $p < .001$, $d = 0.453$.

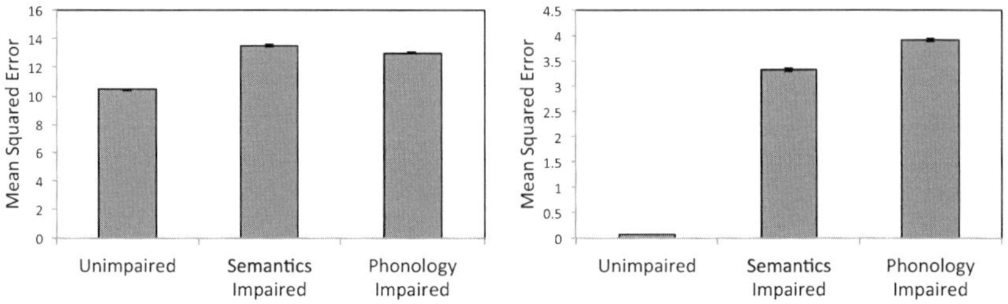

Fig. 5. Performance of the unimpaired, phonological impaired, and semantic impaired models for a reading comprehension task (left) and a reading aloud task (right).

6. Discussion

The fully-implemented triangle model of reading was successful in simulating a broad pattern of behavioral deficits associated with dyslexia, poor-comprehension deficit, and specific language impairment. The model with a phonological deficit had particular difficulty in producing the spoken forms of words, whereas the model with a semantic processing deficit had most difficulty in generating accurate meaning representations for words. This was the case both for the model prior to literacy training, and for the model after it had begun to learn to map orthographic forms onto semantic and phonological representations.

The model was also able to simulate some fine-grained properties of semantic impairment, often associated with specific language impairment. In particular, the model with a semantic processing deficit had particular difficulty in producing the meaning associated with inflectional morphology. This is consistent with the simple view of reading perspective that specific language impairment involves a semantic processing deficit. However, we also found that a phonological processing deficit resulted in impairment to production of meaning associated with inflectional forms, consistent with the modeling work of [9]. This result is also consistent with the simple view of reading that specific language impairment involves also a phonological deficit, though in our simulations the semantic deficit alone resulted in greater impairment. Further simulations could incorporate both a semantic and a phonological processing deficit to determine whether a distinct pattern of behaviour emerges from a phonological processing deficit alone.

One of the most striking features of the results of implementing the simple reading model in the full triangle modeling framework is that an impairment at any point in the network resulted in a suffusing of difficulties throughout the whole reading system. Thus, a semantic processing deficit affected both semantic processing, but also phonological processing in the spoken word comprehension and the spoken word production tasks. Similarly, a phonological processing deficit was also found to affect both these tasks. This is not surprising, however, because both semantic and phonological representations are directly implicated in these tasks. But for the reading comprehension and reading aloud tasks, there was in principle the potential for the model to bypass an impaired representation in learning the task. When learning to map from orthography to phonology, the model could pass activity directly and could also pass activity from orthography to semantics and then to phonology. If the model had a semantic processing deficit, then greater accuracy for a reading aloud task could be achieved by just utilizing the direct route, and reducing the contribution of the indirect route. Similarly, for the reading comprehension task, if the model had a phonological processing deficit, then performance could be enhanced by using just the direct orthography to semantics route, and reducing the activation passing from orthography to phonology and then to semantics.

However, this was not the case in terms of the dynamics of the model, which can be explained in terms of the history of the model's learning. During pretraining, the model had no choice but to attempt to map between phonological and semantic forms, even when a developmental impairment to one of these representational systems was present. This was because no alternative route was available in forming the mapping. The consequence of this pretraining was that the model is unable to "switch off" the contribution of the phonology-semantics subsystem in the triangle model, and this then continued to exert a substantial effect on processing even when more direct routes are available for mapping from orthography.

The model makes a number of predictions for how behaviour translates onto the simple model of reading. The inherent interactivity of the triangle model predicts that processing deficits will never apply purely to only one aspect of reading. A phonological deficit profoundly affects the development and access of semantic representations, and a semantic deficit affects production and stability of phonology. To take one example in terms of behaviour, this means that a phonological processing deficit will primarily affect phonological tasks, such as reading aloud, but should also be observed in the child's development of comprehension. The model shows that the behavioral outcomes of phonological and semantic processing deficits are graded rather than distinct.

The simple model, in terms of its relation to the triangle model, then, requires that the comprehension and the phonological processing dimensions are not orthogonal, but are in fact inter-related. Alternatively, if pure deficits really can be observed in behaviour, then this means that the interactivity within the unconstrained triangle model will need to be reigned in. This parametrisation of an implementation of the simple model of reading requires further information from both behavior, but also from studies of the automaticity of activation of meaning and of phonology for reading comprehension and reading aloud tasks, in children with and without reading impairments.

Acknowledgments

The first author was supported by the Economic and Social Research Council (UK) (grant number ES/L006936/1. The second author was supported by the Economic and Social Research Council (UK) (grant number RES-062-23-3062) and the Rosetrees Trust (grant number A445).

References

1. Bishop, D. V. M., & Snowling, M. J. (2004). Developmental dyslexia and specific language impairment: Same or different? *Psychological Bulletin,* **130**, 858–888.
2. Farmer, R.F. (2000). Issues in the assessment and conceptualization of personality disorders. *Clinical Psychology Review*, **20**, 823-851.
3. Gough, P. B. & Tunmer, W. E. (1986). Decoding, reading, and reading disability. *Remedial and Special Education,* **7**, 6-10.
4. Plaut, D. C., McClelland, J. L., Seidenberg, M. S., & Patterson, K. (1996). Understanding normal and impaired word reading: Computational principles in quasi-regular domains. *Psychological Review*, **103**, 56–115.
5. Perry, C., Ziegler, J. C., & Zorzi, M. (2007). Nested incremental modeling in the development of computational theories: The CDP+ model of reading aloud. *Psychological Review*, **114**, 273-315.
6. McClelland, J.L. (1993). The GRAIN model: a framework for modelling the dynamics of information processing, Meyer, D.E. & Kornblum, S. (Eds.), *Attention and Performance (Vol. XIV): Synergies in Experimental Psychology, Artifical Intelligence, and Cognitive Neuroscience,* pp. 655–688. Mahwah, NJ: Lawrence Erlbaum.
7. Harm, M. W., & Seidenberg, M. S. (1999). Phonology, reading acquisition, and dyslexia: Insights from connectionist models. *Psychological Review*, **106**, 491-528.
8. Joanisse, M. F., & Seidenberg, M. S. (2003). Phonology and syntax in specific language impairment: Evidence from a connectionist model. *Brain and Language*, **86**, 1, 40-56.

9. Joanisse, M. F. (2004). Specific language impairments in children phonology, semantics, and the English past tense. *Current Directions in Psychological Science*, **13**, 4, 156-160.
10. Robertson, E. K., Joanisse, M. F., Desroches, A. S., & Terry, A. (2012). Past-tense morphology and phonological deficits in children with dyslexia and children with language impairment. *Journal of Learning Disabilities*, **46**, 3, 230-240.
11. Harm, M. W., & Seidenberg, M. S. (2004). Computing the meaning of words in reading: Cooperative division of labor between visual and phonological processes. *Psychological Review*, **111**, 662–720.
12. Baayen, R.H., Pipenbrock, R. & Gulikers, L. (1995). *The CELEX Lexical Database* (CD-ROM). Philadelphia, PA: Linguistic Data Consortium, University of Pennsylvania.
13. Miller, G. A. (1990). WordNet: An on-line lexical database. *International Journal of Lexicography*, **3**, 235-312.
14. Thomas, M. S. C. & Karmiloff-Smith, A. (2002). Are developmental disorders like cases of adult brain damage? Implications from connectionist modelling. *Behavioral and Brain Sciences*, **25**, 727-788.

Dynamics of Word Learning in Typically Developing, Temporarily Delayed, and Persistent Late-Talking Children

C. E. Sims*, S. M. Schilling, and E. Colunga
Department of Psychology and Neuroscience, University of Colorado Boulder, Boulder, CO 80303, U.S.A.
**E-mail: ceholtpatrick@colorado.edu*
www.colorado.edu

While typically-developing toddlers learn new words in systematic ways that correspond to their vocabulary structure, late talker children do not. Through a longitudinal study and neural network models, we explore the interactions between attentional biases and vocabulary structure in typically-developing children and different categories of late talkers. Building on previous work, our neural network model shows that, with just vocabulary structure as input, we are able to predict the dynamics of bias interaction around the emergence of the shape bias as observed in typical children. Here we show that, in a population of persistent late talkers, we are not able to accurately predict these dynamics with a model that solely uses vocabulary structure as its input. This suggests that late-talkers may not use the same learning mechanisms to develop attentional biases as do more typical children.

Keywords: Early word learning; Neural networks; Late talkers; Longitudinal.

1. Introduction

Language learning is a crucial milestone of development. Understanding the typical processes of language learning is key to guiding practice and informing research, but it is also important to understand why some children learn "atypically." In the current work, we examine which features typical and late-talker toddlers pay attention to as they learn new words, as a way to gain insight into the phenomenon of word learning in different populations. We combine longitudinal behavioral studies and neural network simulations to investigate differences in the emergence of attentional biases over time in typically-developing and late talker children learning English, elucidating the mechanisms behind their different developmental trajectories.

1.1. *Early word learning*

Evidence in the literature suggests that as children learn certain kinds of words, they also learn patterns or constraints about how those words are used in the world. Two such word learning constraints have been shown to be particularly robust in children's noun learning: the shape bias and the material bias[1-4]. These attentional biases in early word learning are typically studied experimentally using novel noun generalization (NNG) tasks. In this task a child may be taught a novel name for a novel object. Children show a shape bias, extending that novel name to other objects matching the original in shape, even if the shape match differs from the original in texture, color, or size.[1] In contrast, when taught a novel name for a novel non-solid substance children tend to generalize that name to other non-solids that match the original in material only[2,3]. Typically-developing children show a reliable shape bias by 2 years of age[4] whereas the material bias is typically observed slightly later than the shape bias, at 3 years of age.[5] In general, however, there is a correspondence between the structure of children's vocabulary and the emergence of the shape and material bias at the group level[6] that may even account for individual differences[7].

It seems that children generally know these biases, but how do they acquire them? The literature suggests that this is related to the kinds of words children learn as they grow. Results of longitudinal studies have shown that increased attention to shape coincides with increased noun learning, suggesting a relationship between noun learning and bias development[4]. Further, training 17-month-olds on labels for novel shape-based categories both promotes an earlier shape bias and results in a dramatic increase in overall noun vocabulary size compared to a control group[8].

Though in typical development the nouns a child knows and the way the child learns new nouns go hand in hand, this is not the case for all children. Unlike their typically developing counterparts, children who lag in their vocabulary acquisition, so-called *late talkers*, do not systematically extend the name of a novel solid object to other objects that match it in shape[9,10]. In fact, in one study, almost half of the late talkers systematically extended the novel name of a solid object to others matching in texture rather than shape[9]. The decoupling of noun learning and attentional biases may mean that these children learn through different mechanisms. In this paper we look at the dynamics of the emergence of attentional biases in typically-developing and late-talker children and in neural network models.

1.2. *Our approach*

Our previous work has shown that a connectionist network trained on a noun vocabulary structured like that of the average 2-year-old will exhibit kind-specific generalizations akin to those of average 2-year-olds[11]. More recently we have shown that the vocabularies of individual late talkers and early talkers create different word learning biases in our models. These neural networks are identical except for the proportions of words of each type that they are trained on (words referring to solids or non-solids that are alike in shape, material, or both). These models make novel predictions: once fully trained, early talker networks show early shape and material biases, while late talker networks overgeneralize the shape bias to all items[6]. We have confirmed these predictions in toddlers[12, 13].

Identifying the mechanisms behind word learning, particularly delayed word learning, can lead to developing early identification and intervention tools for children's language learning. In the present work, we look at the relationship between vocabulary composition and attentional biases using a longitudinal approach. Although some of the work reviewed above investigated children's development of word learning biases longitudinally[4,8], most look at cross sections along this developmental track. Further, few connectionist models of word learning have implemented a longitudinal approach, capturing an ongoing process of change as it occurs[14,15]. Using longitudinal methodology to study the emergence of word learning biases is unique and can provide insights into how different patterns emerge in different groups of learners. We observe word learning over time in different populations of children and model different learning trajectories using a neural network. In Experiment 1 we examine this relationship in typically developing children, and in Experiment 2 we look at different types of late talkers. If late talkers do learn through the same mechanisms as typical talkers, albeit at a slower pace, we should be able to predict their word learning using the same models which accurately predict typical children's word learning.

2. Experiment 1: Typical word learners

The first experiment charts the development of attentional biases in typically-developing children. We analyze the window of time in which each child begins to show a reliable shape bias, and demonstrate how these children attend to different types of features over time as they reach this word-learning milestone. Subsequently, we model this process by using a typical early vocabulary as input to our network. Thus, the model's ability to capture behavioral patterns should reflect the importance of the structure of a child's vocabulary in their ability to acquire word learning biases.

2.1. *Method*

2.1.1. *Participants*

Participants were selected from a sample of a year-long longitudinal study in which children visited the lab once every month from 18 to 30 months of age. A subset of 12 children were selected for Experiment 1, based on having a typically sized vocabulary, according to norms on the MacArthur-Bates Communicative Development Inventory (MCDI)[16], over the course of the study[a] and showing a reliable shape bias for solid objects within the year of study. The sample included equal numbers of boys and girls with a mean age of 17.2 months at the beginning of the study and 28.8 months at the end.

2.1.2. *Behavioral measures*

We analyzed children's attention in word learning with a novel noun generalization (NNG) task. At each monthly visit to the lab, children completed two NNG tasks, one trial for solid objects and one trial for non-solid substances. There were three different object sets for each type of NNG task; one set was administered at each visit, with object sets cycled at consecutive visits.

In the solid NNG task, children were presented with a novel name for a novel exemplar (e.g., "palo"). Then children were shown five test objects: two objects matching the exemplar in shape, one matching in material, one matching in color, and one matching in both color and material (see left side of Figure 1)[b]. Children were asked, "Can you find another *palo*?" and choices were recorded in order until the child responded "no" or chose all items presented. Performance was measured by the order of children's choices, indicating which features they preferentially attended to. Choices were coded into an attention score with higher values if they were chosen first: the first choice received a score of 3, the second choice a score of 2, the third choice a score of 1; subsequent choices were disregarded. For example, in the solid NNG task a child could have a maximum attention score of 5 if they chose the two shape matches as their first two choices.

---

[a] On average, children were at the 47th percentile on the MCDI at the midpoint of analyses.

[b] An analogous design was used for the non-solid NNG task; see right side of Figure 1.

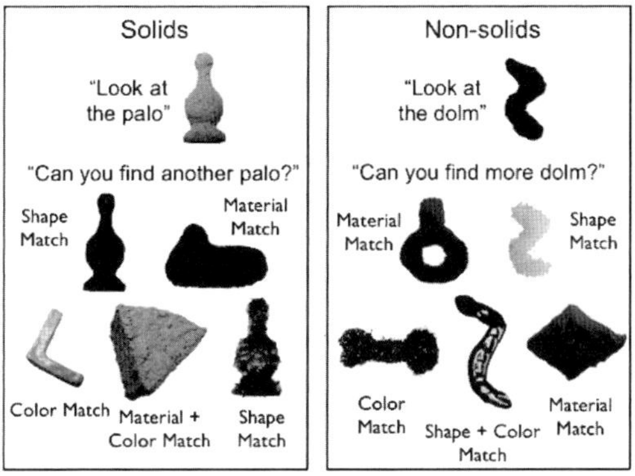

Fig. 1. Example stimuli sets for solid and non-solid NNG tasks.

We used the order of children's choices to observe how children attended to shape and material in the context of solid objects and non-solid substances and to identify the point when children had developed a reliable shape bias. We devised a bias score which takes into account both the extent that children attended to the relevant feature (i.e., shape) as well as the extent to which they excluded irrelevant features (i.e., material). We define the point of shape bias emergence for each child as the point when that child shows the bias (i.e., a bias score surpassing a predetermined criterion value) on three consecutive visits. Analyses were centered around this time point.

2.1.3. *Neural network simulations: Network dynamics*

Our models use the LEABRA algorithm (Local, Error-driven and Associative, Biologically Realistic Algorithm), combining Hebbian learning, which is useful for extracting generalities, and error-driven learning, which hones in on specific, complex patterns. For more details on network dynamics, see [19]. Together, these two algorithms provide a well-suited methodology for investigating how children learn.

2.1.4. *Network architecture*

The architecture is adapted from [11] and is implemented as shown in Figure 2. Words are represented discretely and are input on the Word Layer. Features are represented as distributed patterns over several dimensions on the Perceptual Layer. For example, the shape and material of an object (e.g., the roundness of a particular ball and its yellow rubbery material) are represented by an activation pattern along the Perceptual Layer, with 12 units for shape and 12 units for material[c]. Solidity is represented locally; one unit stands for Solid and another for Non-Solid. Finally, a 25 unit Hidden Layer is connected to all the other layers and to itself. Learning progresses as internal representations, or weights, update and form representations which connect the other two layers, forming associations between the different perceptual features of the word and the word label itself.

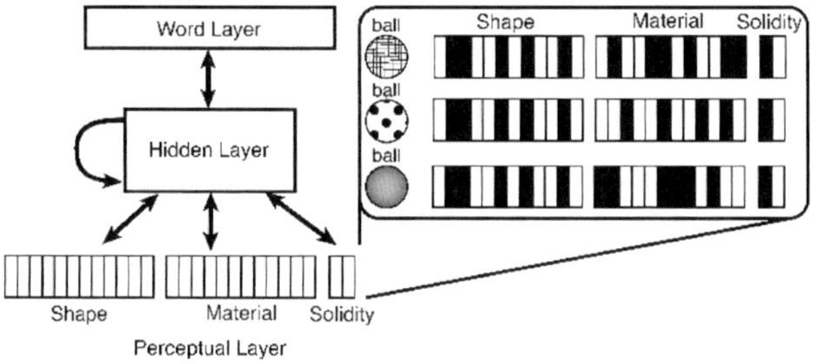

Fig. 2. Network architecture (left) and example input patterns (right).

2.1.5. *Training patterns and procedure*

The training input patterns, adapted from those used in [11], represent the structure of a child's vocabulary. To capture this typical early vocabulary structure, we used the 30-month-old vocabulary norms of the MCDI[16]. We divided the nouns on the MCDI into six categories based on solidity (solid or non-solid) and characteristic feature (shape, material, or both)[d]. Inputs to the model were designed to match these percentages; see Table 1 for an example input vocabulary of a typical talker. The network learning the entire set of training patterns represents a child learning a typical vocabulary.

[c] With 12 binary units for a perceptual feature (i.e. shape), this means that the network has $2^{12} = 4096$ possible shapes (with varying amounts of similarity) it could encounter. This does not necessarily correspond to any possible amount of shapes which a toddler could encounter or perceive in the real world. Rather, this just represents the network having some amount of variability of experience. This number was carried over from the model architecture in [13].

[d] These category divisions were based on adult judgments of solidity and characteristic feature of the words on the MCDI; see [13] for details. Characteristic feature denotes the type of feature that is most distinctive to an item (e.g., all balls are spherical and can be made of different materials, therefore the distinctive feature of the category *ball* is shape).

Table 1. Noun categories based on adult judgments of solidity and characteristic feature. Percentages indicate category representations for a typical 30-month-old vocabulary. An example noun from each category is also provided

	Characteristic Shape	Characteristic Material	Both
Solid	51%	7%	35%
	ball	*chalk*	*penny*
Non-Solid	0%	4%	3%
	bubble	*milk*	*jeans*

2.2. *Results*

2.2.1. *Behavioral results*

The dependent measure of attention in word learning was children's coded choices (i.e., their attention scores) in the NNG tasks. We analyzed attention to shape match objects on solid testing trials and attention to material matches on non-solid trials. Therefore, there were two attention score values calculated at each time point.

Attention to characteristic feature scores were submitted to a linear mixed models (LMM) analysis with time (before, at, or after shape bias emergence), trial type (shape solid or material-nonsolid), and the interaction between time and trial type as predictor variables. Trial type was a significant predictor of attention scores, with children attending to shape on solid trials relatively more ($M = 3.36$, $SD = 1.73$) than to material on non-solid trials ($M = 2.25$, $SD = 1.65$; $F(1, 60) = 10.02$, $p < .01$). The interaction between time and trial type was also a significant predictor of children's attention scores ($F(2, 60) = 9.51$, $p < .001$).

As can be seen in Figure 3A, as children developed a shape bias, they attended more to shape on solid test trials. This can be seen in a significant increase from the time point before to the point of emergence ($t(11) = 3.93$, $p < .01$). This pattern is expected based on the definition of the shape bias; of particular interest is how children attend to material relative to shape during this time. At the point of shape bias emergence, children's attention to shape on solid trials was significantly higher than their attention to material on non-solid trials ($t(11) = 7.35$, $p < .001$). However, at the other two time points, there was no difference in attention to shape compared to material.

2.2.2. *Network simulation results*

The dependent measure was proportion of characteristic feature choices at each testing trial in the networks (shape on solid trials, material on non-solid trials).

These proportions were submitted to an LMM analysis with three predictor variables: time (before, at, or after shape bias emergence), trial type (shape solid or material non-solid), and their interaction. Time was a significant predictor of choice in the networks, with an overall increase in correct characteristic feature choices on both trial types over the emergence of the shape bias ($F(2, 75) = 8.10$, $p = .001$). There was an effect of trial type, with the networks showing more correct shape choices on solid trials relative to material choices on non-solid trials ($F(1, 75) = 12.12$, $p = .001$). The interaction between time and trial type was also significant ($F(2, 75) = 44.74$, $p < .001$).

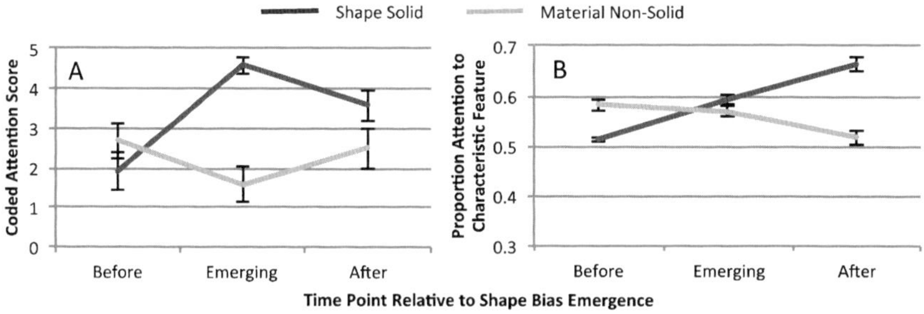

Fig. 3. A. Children's coded attention scores on the NNG task over the emergence of the shape bias. B. Network simulation attention to characteristic features in the virtual NNG task over emergence of the shape bias.

As can be seen in Figure 3B, the relationship between the networks' shape solid choices and material non-solid choices changed over time. Post hoc t-tests showed that shape solid choices increased as the networks developed a shape bias. This increase was significant both from the time point before to the point of emergence ($t(14) = 8.85$, $p < .001$) as well as from emergence to the point after ($t(14) = 6.34$, $p < .001$). Over this same time period, material non-solid choices decreased, particularly from the point of shape bias emergence to the point after ($t(14) = 3.86$, $p < .01$). While the networks showed a significantly higher amount of material non-solid choices relative to shape solid choices prior to developing a shape bias ($t(14) = 6.08$, $p < .001$), this relationship is reversed at the time point after shape bias emergence ($t(14) = 6.28$, $p < .001$).

2.3. *Discussion*

The behavioral results from children add new insights into effects reported in the literature. As children developed an attentional bias to shape in learning names for solid objects they showed relatively diminished attention to material in the context of non-solids. Changes to attention and learning based on one particular feature seem to entail a tradeoff in attention to other features.

Further, the neural network results replicate and add to prior findings: The vocabulary structure of a typical toddler is sufficient to support the development of attentional biases during word learning. They also capture the interaction effects seen in the child data. Of note, the patterns of the interaction differ somewhat between the networks and children, particularly after the emergence of the shape bias. This may suggest that once children attain a stable shape bias, they no longer need to increase attention to shape to reap the benefits in vocabulary learning and attention can instead shift to focus on other features, like material. In contrast, once the network begins to hone in on a feature, it may continue that focus until all relevant items from the input are learned. We will further discuss the implications of these results in the general discussion; next we turn to late talkers.

3. Experiment 2: Late talkers

In the second experiment we identified three subgroups of late talkers based on the persistence of their delay. In Experiment 1, we used the neural network model to show that the vocabulary structure of typically-developing children alone was enough to capture the dynamics of attentional biases in a longitudinal sample of typically developing children. Here we document the development of attentional biases in different groups of late talkers. We again compare behavioral findings to model predictions to answer the question: to what extent does the vocabulary structure of late talkers account for the dynamics of the emergence of their word learning biases?

3.1. *Method*

3.1.1. *Participants*

Participants were selected from the same longitudinal study as in Experiment 1. In Experiment 2, we focused on children at or below the 30th percentile on the MCDI at their first visit to the lab (N = 33, 15 boys and 18 girls, M_{age} = 17.5 months).

These late talkers were divided into groups by their vocabulary learning over time. Children who were no longer in the late talker range by their sixth visit were grouped together as non-persistent late talkers (N = 18). Children who were still in the late talker range at visit 6 but who were out of the range by visit 12 were grouped as short-term persistent late talkers ($N = 10$). Finally, children who remained in the late talker range from the first through twelfth visit were grouped as long-term persistent late talkers ($N = 5$).

3.1.2. *Behavioral measures and neural network simulation*

We tracked attention in word learning as described in Experiment 1, namely using NNG tasks. Because the late talkers in the study did not all consistently reach a shape bias within the year of participation, we could not center our analyses around the emergence of the shape bias. Instead, we analyzed late talkers over a fixed time period, from their first through sixth visits.

The models were the same as in Experiment 1, except for the input vocabulary used to train the network. Here, we used the vocabulary structures of each late talker child (collected monthly with the MCDI) as input to the model. As they trained on the late talker vocabularies, the networks were tested on the same virtual NNG task as in Experiment 1.

3.2. *Results*

3.2.1. *Behavioral results*

The dependent measure of attention in word learning was children's coded choices in the NNG tasks. Initial inspection of the data by visit, trial type, and late talker group showed highly variable data (see Figure 4A) and no interactions involving talker group. For a more focused analysis, we averaged over visit (see Figure 4B). We examined group patterns over visits to identify trends in the data. Across all time points, there was a trend in which long-term persistent late talkers showed less of a difference between attention to shape on solid trials and attention to material on non-solid trials compared to the other two late talker groups (see Figure 4B). Specifically, ANOVA results showed both the non-persistent ($F(1, 12) = 20.06$, $p < .001$) and short-term persistent ($F(1, 4) = 17.06$, $p = .01$) groups showed significant effects of trial type, whereas the long-term persistent group did not ($p > .10$).

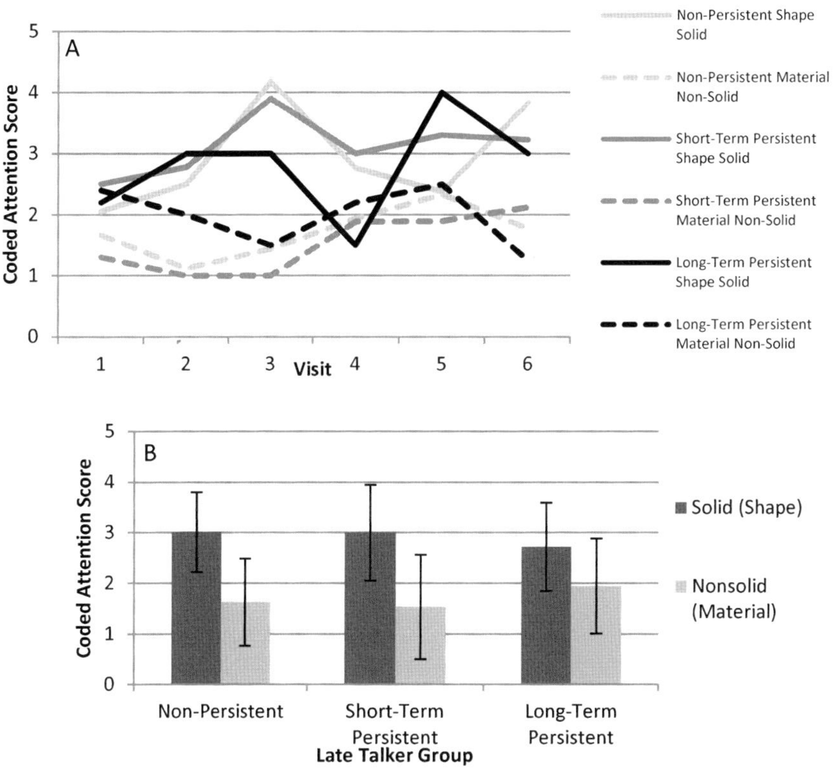

Fig. 4. A. Children's coded attention scores in the NNG task by group and trial type over time. B. Children's coded attention scores averaged across all visits.

3.2.2. *Network simulation results*

The dependent measure was proportion of characteristic feature choices at each testing trial in the networks. Proportions of feature choices were submitted to an LMM analysis with visit (7 virtual visits[e]), trial type (shape solid or material non-solid), late talker group (non-persistent, short-term persistent, and long-term persistent), and their interactions included as predictors. Time was a significant predictor of choice in the networks, with an overall increase in characteristic feature choices over time ($F(1, 30) = 1272.44$, $p < .0001$). There was also an effect of trial type ($F(1, 390) = 4.88$, $p < .05$), however as can be seen in Figure 5A, the interaction between time and trial type was also a significant predictor in

[e] The network has seven, rather than six, time points of analysis because we included a preliminary point in training at which the weights were initialized.

the model ($F(1, 390) = 1138.34$, $p < .0001$). Increases in attention were large in the context of shape for solids and modest in the context of material for non-solids. Additionally, talker type ($F(2, 390) = 13.33$, $p < .0001$) and the interaction between talker type and trial type ($F(2, 390) = 8.97$, $p < .001$) were also significant. As seen in Figure 5A the long-term persistent group diverged from the other two groups in the solid-shape trials, showing relatively higher proportions of shape choices.

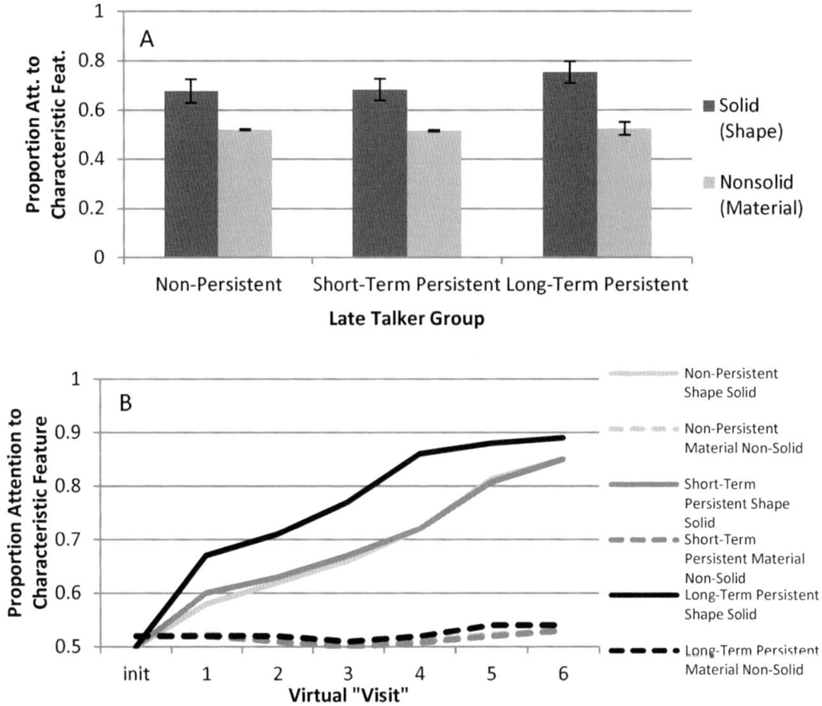

Fig. 5. A. Network simulation attention to characteristic features in the virtual NNG task over visits. B. Network simulation attention averaged over all time points.

3.3. *Discussion*

Though the data in Figure 4A appears to look the same across all groups, the behavioral results of Experiment 2 revealed that different types of late talkers show different word learning patterns around shape bias emergence; Non-persistent and short-term persistent late talkers were similar in the development of attentional biases. Long-term persistent late talkers stood out from the other groups. The current data does not include a large sample, so this statistical difference could be further supported by collecting more data.

Network results were consistent with behavioral results in non-persistent and short-term persistent late talkers in that shape was chosen more in solid trials than material in non-solid trials, as shown by significant effects of trial type. However, we see a difference in the behavioral results compared to the network results in long-term persistent late talkers. Behavioral results showed that long-term persistent late talkers chose shape in solid trials at statistically the same rate as material in non-solid trials. In the networks, we see the opposite trend, with an interaction between talker type and trial type: long-term persistent networks chose shape in solid trials more than non-persistent or short-term persistent networks, yet all groups chose material in non-solid trials to the same extent. This further sets apart long-term persistent late talkers and suggests that other factors aside from vocabulary structure have an influence on attentional bias learning for this particular population of children.

4. General discussion

The two experiments presented here explored word learning patterns of different populations of children and investigated how a neural network model can capture different learning trajectories. The first experiment showed that in toddlers with typically developing vocabularies, there are interactions in the development of attentional biases in novel word learning. As children developed a shape bias, their attention to material in the context of non-solid substances waned. Our model of word learning captured a similar interaction pattern, although with some differences in time course of changes. In short, the network captures the general pattern of bias interaction observed in children, and demonstrates the role of vocabulary structure in shaping these trajectories.

The second experiment showed that attentional bias patterns differed depending on the trajectory of a child's vocabulary. Children who were long-term late talkers showed distinct patterns compared to temporary late talkers. When it came to novel word learning, the long-term persistent group showed a trend of having less distinct biases. That is, the other two late talker groups showed an appreciably higher degree of attention to shape on solid trials than attention to material on non-solid trials than long-term persistent late talkers.

Perhaps the most important take away point from these results, however, is the discrepancy in the model's ability to predict bias learning in different populations of children. With the sole varying input being vocabulary structure, the model predicts the bias interactions observed in typical talkers and temporary late talkers. However, it was unable to capture the bias learning of long-term persistent late talkers, suggesting that their language learning may rely on different learning mechanisms. These children may need to utilize other information such as social cues or repeated exposure in order to fully learn the words. A follow-up experiment could test this same set of children in a different word learning context, where, for instance, the experimenter provides social cues such as eye contact and observing whether children who are long-term persistent late-talkers can effectively leverage this information in word learning. Investigating children who learn words differently is an important direction for research to better understand how all children learn and what can be done for each child to improve his or her learning. For now, this paper shows that long-term persistent late-talkers may learn through a different mechanism than most children and identifies this is a topic for future investigation.

Acknowledgments

This research was supported by NICHD grant R01 HD067315 to Eliana Colunga.

References

1. B. Landau, L. B. Smith, & S. S. Jones, The importance of shape in early lexical learning, *Cog. Dev.* **3**, 299 (1988).
2. N. N. Soja, Inferences about the meaning of nouns: The relationship between perception and syntax, *Cog. Dev.* **7(1)**, 29 (1992).
3. N. N. Soja, S. Carey, & E. S. Spelke, Ontological categories guide young children's inductions of word meanings: Object terms and substance terms *Cognition*, **38(2)**, 179 (1991).
4. L. Gershkoff-Stowe & L. B. Smith, Shape and the first hundred nouns, *Child Dev.* **75**, 1098 (2004).
5. H. Yoshida & L. B. Smith, Linguistic cues enhance the learning of perceptual cues, *Psych. Science*, **16**, 90 (2005).
6. E. Colunga & C. E. Sims, Early talkers and late talkers know nouns that license different word learning biases, in *Proc. of the 33rd Annual Conf. of the Cog. Sci. Society* (Boston, MA, 2011).
7. L. K. Perry & L. K. Samuelson, The shape of the vocabulary predicts the shape of the bias, *Frontiers in Psych.* **2**, 345 (2011).
8. L. B. Smith, S. S. Jones, B. Landau, L. Gershkoff-Stowe, & L. K. Samuelson, Creating a shape bias creates rapid word learners, *Psych. Sci.* **13**, 13 (2002).

9. S. S. Jones, Late talkers show no shape bias in a novel name extension task, *Dev. Sci.* **6**, 477 (2003).
10. B. A. Collisson, B. Grela, T. Spaulding, J. G. Ruecki, & J. S. Magnuson, Individual differences in the shape bias in preschool children with specific language impairment and typical language development: theoretical and clinical implications, *Dev. Sci.* (2014).
11. E. Colunga & L. B. Smith, From the lexicon to expectations about kinds: A role for associative learning, *Psych. Rev.* **112**, 347 (2005).
12. E. Colunga & C. E. Sims, Early-talker and late-talker toddlers and networks show different word learning biases, in *Proc. of the 34th Annual Conf. of the Cog. Sci. Society* (Sapporo, Japan, 2012).
13. E. Colunga & C. E. Sims, Not only size matters: early-talker and late-talker vocabularies support different word learning biases in babies and networks, (under review).
14. B. McMurray, J. S. Horst, L. K. Samuelson, Word learning emerges from the interaction of online referent selection and slow associative learning, *Psych. Rev.* **119**, 831 (2012).
15. T. Regier, The emergence of words: Attentional learning in form and meaning, *Cog. Sci.* **29**, 819 (2005).
16. L. Fenson, P. Dale, J. S. Reznick, D. Thal, E. Bates, J. Hartung, S. Pethick, & J. S. Reilly, *The MacArthur Communicative Development Inventories: User's Guide and Technical Manual* (Paul H. Brokes, Baltimore, 1993).
17. R. C. O'Reilly, Y. Munakata, M. J. Frank, & T. E. Hazy, *Computational Cognitive Neuroscience.* Wiki Book, 1st Edition. URL: http://ccnbook.colorado.edu (2012).

Complex Word Recognition Behaviour Emerges from the Richness of the Word Learning Environment

Alastair C. Smith
Max Planck Institute for Psycholinguistics, Wundtlaan 1, Nijmegen, Netherlands.
E-mail: alastair.smith@mpi.nl

Padraic Monaghan
Department of Psychology, Lancaster University, Lancaster LA1 4YF, United Kingdom

Falk Huettig
Max Planck Institute for Psycholinguistics, Wundtlaan 1, Nijmegen, Netherlands

Computational models can reflect the complexity of human behaviour by implementing multiple constraints within their architecture, and/or by taking into account the variety and richness of the environment to which the human is responding. We explore the second alternative in a model of word recognition that learns to map spoken words to visual and semantic representations of the words' concepts. Critically, we employ a phonological representation utilising coarse-coding of the auditory stream, to mimic early stages of language development that are not dependent on individual phonemes to be isolated in the input, which may be a consequence of literacy development. The model was tested at different stages during training, and was able to simulate key behavioural features of word recognition in children: a developing effect of semantic information as a consequence of language learning, and a small but earlier effect of phonological information on word processing. We additionally tested the role of visual information in word processing, generating predictions for behavioural studies, showing that visual information could have a larger effect than semantics on children's performance, but that again this affects recognition later in word processing than phonological information. The model also provides further predictions for performance of a mature word recognition system in the absence of fine-coding of phonology, such as in adults who have low literacy skills. The model demonstrated that such phonological effects may be reduced but are still evident even when multiple distractors from various modalities are present in the listener's environment. The model demonstrates that complexity in word recognition can emerge from a simple associative system responding to the interactions between multiple sources of information in the language learner's environment.

Keywords: Speech comprehension; Visual attention; Multimodal processing; Visual world paradigm; Spoken word recognition.

1. Introduction

One of the key aims of computational models is to provide an abstract characterization of a task, in order to determine which cognitive processes may be required in order to simulate observed behaviour. Consideration of the richness of the environment around the cognitive system can produce surprisingly complex behavior as a result of the operation of only very simple internal cognitive processes. Thus, the complexity is in the world, rather than (or as well as) within the system itself.

Yet, decisions not only about what to include, but also what to exclude, in representing the input to the system clearly have huge implications for the validity of the computational model, and also its relevance to the actual task in hand. Language processing is one such domain where input has often been isolated to a single abstracted modality of representation – usually auditory input to the system[7,15,28]. Thus, language models take as input streams of sound, usually pre-segmented into linguistically interpretable units (such as phonemes, morphemes or words) and then test the effect of environmental exposure to this linguistic information on learning mappings to other assumed linguistic representations of language, such as the written form of the word (for a task associated with literacy)[10], or to the meaning of the word (for tasks such as auditory word comprehension)[9], or even a syntactic or discourse structure (for processing of sentences or utterances)[8].

However, in our recent modelling, we have been examining the interacting role of multimodal information sources on language processing, and we have discovered that this interaction is critical to a full appreciation of how the language processing system operates in situ. We have been exploring a model of single word processing that takes into account not only the phonological representations of words, but also the word's meaning, and visual objects present in the environment of the language learner as they acquire their language[18,24,25]. Rather than just considering mapping between pairs of representations, as in classic models of language processing[9,10,17,20,21,22], we have investigated how auditory, visual, and semantic information about words inter-relates in word processing. This has been advantageous for two reasons. First, it has uncovered the nuanced interactions between sources of information and the way in which information integration adjusts over time. The time scales have been both in terms of developmental time, as the model learns more and more words, but also in terms of how a single word processing trial unfolds. Second, the modeling has enabled us to test the role of each type of representational input in the language system's processing without necessarily requiring those representations to be directly involved in the task.

Phonological awareness tasks have frequently been used as tools for probing the structure of representations activated by the speech signal, which interface with the broader language processing system[4]. Phonological awareness can be defined as the ability to manipulate the phonological structure of spoken words. Typical tasks used to assess phonological awareness comprise tests of participants' ability to explicitly adjust the sequence of phonemes in the word[14]. One example is phoneme isolation tasks, where participants are required, for instance, to report the third phoneme in a word. An alternative is a phoneme deletion task, where participants have to report a word or non-word phoneme sequence with one sound removed, e.g., what is "facts" without the /t/ sound.

Phoneme awareness is a major predictor of literacy outcomes, with good performance highly correlated with vocabulary size, reading level, later reading comprehension, and is also an early indicator of developmental dyslexia[2,5,6,14]. Phoneme awareness is also associated with the effect of literacy[30] on the language processing system[23]. Literates in alphabetic languages demonstrate more accomplished phoneme awareness performance than those who have low-literacy or no literacy skills[1,19]. Thus, phoneme awareness, though a predictor of literacy outcomes, is also shown to be at least partially a consequence of literacy development itself. One problem with phoneme awareness tasks is that the phonological representation has to be explicitly manipulated. Thus, it is not only a test of the phonological representation but also the speaker's meta-cognitive ability to manipulate this representation.

An alternative way to assess changes in phonological representation without also requiring direct explicit access to that representation, is to test the effect of phonological processing on other language processing tasks. Huettig, Singh, and Mishra[13] did precisely this, by determining the effect of literacy on processing spoken word input on activation of words with overlapping phonological representations. The extent of the overlap clarifies the granularity of the listener's phonological representation during word processing, where if there is overlap of a single phoneme then sensitivity to this overlap indicates a phoneme-level representation of the input. As an outcome measure, Huettig *et al.*[13] presented the listener with a set of objects, one of which was named by a word similar in sound to the auditory input, one of which was named by a word with similar meaning to the auditory input, and two distractor objects, which were unrelated in sound or meaning to the heard word. The time-course of eye-movements to the phonologically-related, or the semantically-related word indicated the extent to which phonology[3] and semantics[11,29] were affecting word processing at different points in the unfolding of the speech signal. They found that both high-literacy and low-literacy participants looked to the semantically-related object more than to the distractor objects, but that only the high-literacy participants looked more to the phonologically-related object. Furthermore, this phonological effect was observed at an earlier point in the word processing than the semantic effects for the high-literacy individuals. In a second experiment low-literates were shown to display a phonological effect when scenes contained a single phonologically related item accompanied by unrelated distractors but unlike literates this effect was weak, late and pro-longed. This suggested that the low-literacy participants were less able to access the individual phonemes within the word during auditory word processing, thus providing an indirect measure of phonological awareness.

Smith, Monaghan, and Huettig[25] constructed a multimodal language processing model that aimed to simulate the cognitive effects of literacy on phonological representations for visual world language processing tasks. The model is illustrated in Figure 1. The model has a central processing resource, which is connected to and from a variety of modalities that can be inputs and/or outputs to the language processing system. In Figure 1, visual, phonological, and semantic information is indicated, and the output of the model is a set of units representing the fixation position of the eye. Two versions of the model were compared. The first was able to process the individual phonemes in the word as the auditory input unfolded over time. The second was able only to process at a coarser granularity, with syllables, or whole words, rather than individual phonemes processed from the input. The model with phoneme-level representations was able to simulate both the later semantically-related and the early phonologically-related influences on eye movements displayed by literates. The model with syllable-level representations simulated the later semantically-related effects and weaker, prolonged phonological effects displayed by illiterates. Thus, the model showed that the effects of literacy on visual world language processing were consistent with changes from coarse- to fine-coding representations of the word's phonology.

The developmental trajectory of the same multimodal model's processing was also investigated[27]. In this simulation, we investigated the simultaneous involvement of phonological, semantic, and visual information in auditory word processing. The same model as shown in Figure 1 was trained to learn to link auditory representations, that were akin to the fine-grained phoneme representations in the literacy simulations, to visual and semantic representations of words. After training, the model was tested on its eye-movement simulated behaviour when presented with visual scenes comprising a phonologically-related object, a semantically-related object, a visually-similar object, and an unrelated object. The model was able to simulate the temporal order of all three effects in adult word processing: an effect of phonology early in word processing, and then a later effect of semantic and visual relatedness. Analysis of semantic activity in the model indicated that early phonological effects were partly driven by activation of the semantic properties of the phonologically-related object at levels similar to that of the target during periods in the unfolding of the spoken word in which the phonology overlapped.

The development of these effects as the model learned gradually to map between each of the individual representations, in a simulation of vocabulary development, was also consistent with patterns of phonological, semantic, and visual processing in early and later childhood. Mani and Huettig[16] tested children aged 2, 4, 6, and 8 years old on word processing when viewing a phonologically-related, a semantically-related and two unrelated distractor pictures. They found that semantic effects increased with age, whereas phonologically-related effects became more stable as age increased, altering from a long-lasting effect after the word had been spoken, to resemble more closely adult performance, with a more focused phonological processing effect occurring closer in time to the word's spoken production.

However, these developmental simulations were, as mentioned, conducted with a fine-coding phonological representation where speech was represented as a sequence of individuated phonemes, whereas this is unlikely to occur at earlier stages of word learning, such as ages 2 and 4 years old, with children only beginning to transition to phoneme grain-size representations at or after onset of formal literacy (e.g., ages 6 and 8 years old).

In this chapter we report simulations to test whether it is possible to simulate the developmental effects of multimodal processing during word recognition when a more realistic, coarse-coding representation of phonology is initially available to the model. A further issue explored by the simulations in this chapter is to generate predictions about how the effects of phonological, semantic, and visual-relatedness unfold over a single trial in low-literacy participants who do not have fine-grained phoneme level representations of phonology. Previously, effects of literacy in visual world language processing tasks have not also included visually-related objects, and these have been shown to dramatically reduce observable effects of phonological relatedness[26]. Thus far, participants with low-literacy have not been tested on the relative role of visual processing in the visual world paradigm and so the current simulations provide also predictions for future behavioural investigations.

2. Modelling multimodal language development

2.1. *Method*

2.1.1. *Architecture*

The model is similar to that employed in Smith *et al.*[27], and illustrated in Figure 1. The model comprised several modalities connecting to a set of 400 hidden units in an integrative layer: a set of 80 visual units, with 20 units each associated with one of four object positions in the visual environment; a set of 60 phonological units representing the spoken form of a monosyllabic word; and 200 semantic units, to represent the word's meaning. The integrative, hidden layer was self-connected, and also projected to the semantic layer. This was in order that the model could also generate semantic representations, and not only use semantic information as an input source. As output from the model, there was a set of four units, each representing one of four visual object positions, to which the eye could be directed. This eye layer was also connected back to the integrative layer. The eye layer enabled a read-off of the model's behaviour regarding simulating eye-movement behavioural experiments using the visual world paradigm.

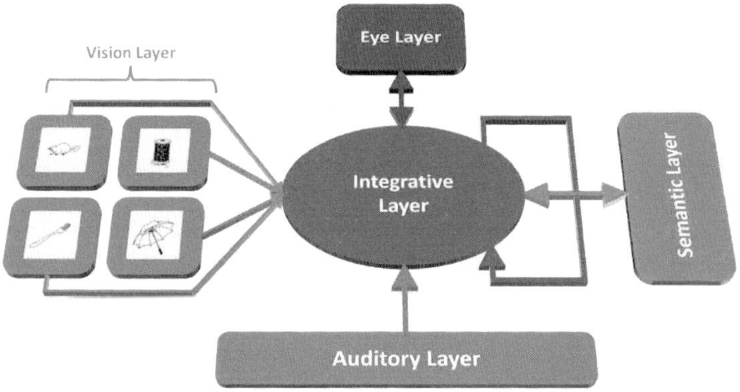

Fig. 1. Architecture of the Multimodal Integration Model of language processing (MIM).

2.1.2. *Training and testing*

There were 200 items altogether, each with a unique visual, semantic, and phonological representation. Each visual object representation was composed of 20 units, 10 representing low spatial frequency and 10 representing high spatial frequency visual features. Each unit was active with probability of 0.5. For the semantic representation, a randomly selected unique set of eight units were active for each different word. For the phonological representation, this was encoded at the syllable level, so each word was represented as a unique pattern over a set of 60 units, with each unit active with probability 0.5. This differed from simulations of the model where phonology was encoded at the phoneme level, with a unique pattern distributed over 10 units representing each phoneme and each word encoded by a unique combination of 6 phonemes in the input[27]. Thus, the current simulations were a coarser-coding of the auditory input than fine-grained, phoneme-level representations that have been used to simulate word processing in participants who have phoneme-level awareness of speech stimuli.

To construct stimuli to mimic the visual world paradigm tasks, we generated representations for a subset of words that were related in terms of their visual, semantic, or phonological properties. Within the 200 items were embedded 80 competitor and unrelated distractor items that were controlled for their relationships to 20 target items. This included twenty visual competitors (which each shared their low-spatial frequency visual features with a target item), twenty semantic competitors (which shared 4 of their 8 active semantic features with a target), and 20 phonological competitors, (each of whose phonological pattern was identical to 50% of the yoked target's phonological pattern, while the remainder overlapped randomly). Twenty unrelated distractors were also constructed that were designed to have minimal overlap in visual, semantic and phonological dimensions (see Smith *et al.*[25], for more details).

The model was trained to learn to map between each pair of modalities, in order to simulate the model's development of learning relationships between representations. Thus, for a vision to meaning mapping, simulating an object recognition task, the model was given a visual object representation at one of the four possible visual positions (the location of the object in the visual field was randomised across training trials) and the eye layer unit corresponding to its location was fully activated. The system was then required to learn to activate the semantic pattern corresponding to that object. Similarly, for phonology to semantic mapping a phonological input was provided and random noise as input to the visual layer, with the system required to activate its corresponding semantic pattern. For a phonology to vision mapping, in an object naming task, the model was presented with the phonological input and four different objects in each of the four visual positions randomly selected from the training set (which included all competitors and unrelated distractors), and was required to activate the eye position associated with the target object. The same procedure but with a semantic input rather than a phonological input, was used to train mapping from semantics to vision. For each trial there were 15 time steps, where the input was presented at time step 1, then the model had a further 14 steps in order to activate the other representations associated with the word, and to generate an activation in the eye movement units. The relative activation of each eye position, associated with one of the locations in the visual field of containing a distractor, enabled an assessment of the model's activation of phonological, visual, and semantic information during word recognition.

The model was trained for 1,000,000 separate training trials, and the model's performance was assessed at 250,000 intervals to simulate developmental stages of word learning. The learning rate was 0.05, and weights in the model were adjusted using recurrent backpropagation after each trial, with error computed as the mean squared difference between the actual and target output at the last time step of the trial. Results were averaged over 8 instantiations of the model.

During testing, the model was presented with a simulation of the visual world paradigm, whereby the phonology of a word was presented to the model (time steps 5 - 15), along with a set of objects presented at the visual input (time steps 1 - 15). The objects in the visual display represented the phonologically-related, visually-related, and semantically-related patterns, along with an unrelated distractor item. There were in total 480 testing trials, with 24 different arrangements of object location for each of the 20 words that had an overlapping phonological, semantic, and visual pattern.

The model's performance was assessed by determining the eye-movement over the 15 time steps of the training trial with an additional 15 time steps added to discern further the time-course of activation of the different representational modalities. The influence of overlap in each representational modality was appraised by determining the strength of activation of the eye unit corresponding to the phonologically, semantically, or visually related object, relative to activation of the eye unit corresponding to the unrelated object. We additionally recorded the cosine-distance between activation in the semantic layer and the semantic representations corresponding to each item in the display and the spoken target word in order to examine its relationship to fixation behavior.

In this simulation, we explored two broad aspects of the data. First, we wanted to examine the extent to which the model was able to simulate developmental effects of a growing contribution of semantic information with experience, and also to determine whether, in the model, the emerging early effects of the phonological distractor were evident as a consequence of literacy – so a change from coarse-coding to fine-coding. Discovering that the early phonological distractor effect is not evident in the model at the end of training would be an indication that literacy is required before phonological distractors can exert an effect. However, if the model can demonstrate an early effect of the phonological distractor then this indicates that it is experience rather than a literacy-related qualitative change that can induce the observed behavioural effects. Furthermore, previous developmental behavioural data is based on tests including just a phonological and semantic distractor, so the model enables a further prediction of the role of visual distractors in processing.

Second, we wanted to examine whether the model could reproduce previous findings of a semantic distractor effect, with only a very small phonological distractor effect, in low-literates[13,25], i.e., with proposed coarse-coding of phonological input, when a visual distractor was also present. This, too, was a novel investigation of the task as previous simulations and behavioural studies had not tested the effect of also including visually-related distractors in the display. In this case, we also wanted to explore the time-course of fixation to the visual distractor, to generate predictions about how such multiple modalities might influence word recognition performance in a low-literacy population.

2.2. *Results*

The model's performance was assessed at each of the four developmental stages, with fixation of phonologically related, semantically related, visually related and unrelated objects tracked as the trial unfolded. The results are shown in Figure 2.

Early in development, after 250,000 training trials, the model demonstrated no significant eye movement activation to any of the related distractors relative to the unrelated distractor, all $|t| \leq 1.130$, all $p \geq .296$.

However, from 500,000 trials onwards, the model demonstrated a growing semantic distractor effect. For 500,000 trials, the semantic distractor resulted in a higher activation than the unrelated distractor from time step 15 through to the end of the trial at time step 30, all $|t| \geq 2.641$, all $p \leq .033$, with a maximum ratio difference of 1.745, meaning that the semantic distractor position resulted in 1.745 times the activation than the unrelated distractor. For 750,000 trials, the effect was larger and earlier, beginning at time step 14, all $|t| \geq 2.693$, all $p \leq .031$, with maximum ratio of 2.285, It was earlier still, from time step 13, after 1,000,000 training trials, all $|t| \geq 2.648$, all $p \leq .033$, but the maximum ratio of 2.054 was no greater than after 750,000 trials.

In terms of activation of phonology, the model showed an effect of the phonological distractor from 500,000 trials, with activation of the eye position associated with the phonologically-related object greater than that of the unrelated distractor from time step 13, all $|t| \geq 2.434$, all $p \leq .045$, maximum ratio = 1.410. After 750,000 trials, the effect was earlier, from time step 12, all $|t| \geq 2.513$, all $p \leq .040$, maximum ratio = 1.667, and after 1,000,000 trials, it continued to be significant from time step 12, all $|t| \geq 2.630$, all $p \leq .034$, with maximum ratio =

1.525. Interestingly, as for the simulations in Smith et al.[27] using a fine-coding of the phonological input, the model demonstrated a prolonged effect of phonological relatedness, which was consistent with the developmental data, but not with adult performance for such visual world tasks. Furthermore, as in the developmental behavioural data, the phonological effect was substantially smaller than that of the semantic effect (as seen in Figure 2, panels B, C and D).

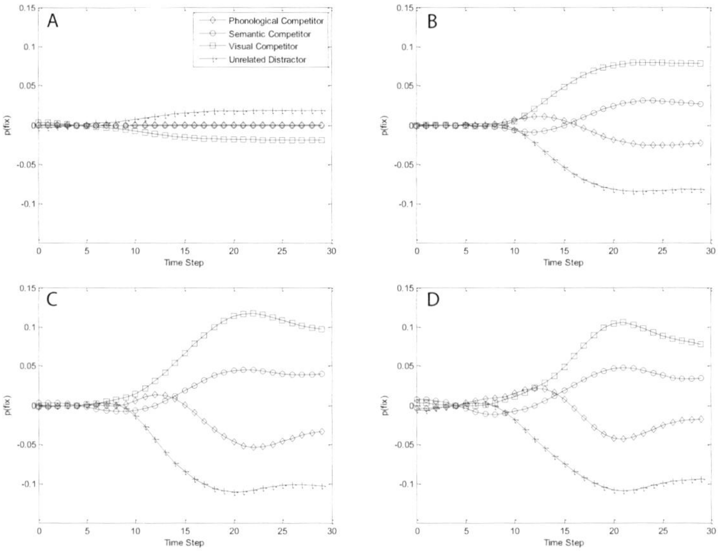

Fig. 2. The MIM model's performance on phonological, semantic, and visual distractor stimuli, compared against an unrelated distractor, across 30 time steps of a single trial. A after 250,000 training patterns; B after 500,000 training patterns; C after 750,000 training patterns; and D after 1,000,000 training patterns.

For the novel predictions of the visual representation effects, these were also observable from mid- to late-stages of development of the model. After 500,000 trials, there was a significant effect of the visual distractor from time step 14 onwards, all $|t| \geq 3.045$ all $p \leq .019$, maximum ratio = 2.051. After 750,000 trials, the effect was earlier and larger, from time step 13, all $|t| \geq 2.891$, all $p \leq .023$, maximum ratio = 2.966. Further training resulted in an earlier and more reliable difference, from time step 12, all $|t| \geq 3.996$, all $p \leq .005$, but not a larger effect: maximum ratio = 2.539.

The mean cosine similarity between semantic layer activity and the semantic representations of each of the visually displayed objects and the spoken target word was calculated at each time step within test trials performed by networks after 1,000,000 training trials. The difference from this measure calculated at word onset (time step 5) for all subsequent time steps is displayed in Figure 3 in addition to the level of activation of eye layer units corresponding to each category of object in the visual display. These data indicated strong activation of the semantic properties of both the semantically related object and the spoken target word but little activation of the semantic properties of the visually related object, the phonologically related object and the unrelated object. This contrasts with simulations in Smith et al.[27] using a fine-coding of the phonological input which showed early strong activation of the semantic properties of the phonological competitor.

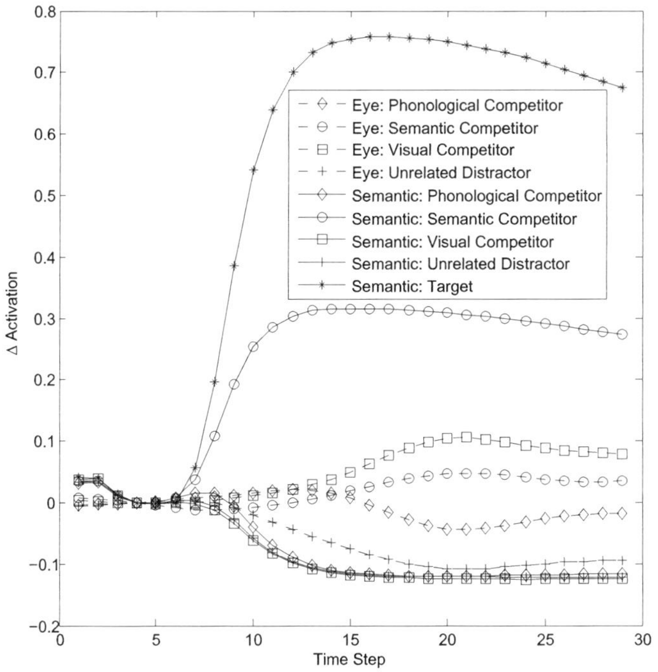

Fig. 3. Change in semantic layer and eye layer activity from word onset in the MIM model after 1,000,000 training patterns across 30 time steps of a single trial simulating visual world conditions with scenes containing a phonological, a semantic, a visual and an unrelated distractor. [Eye = activation of eye layer unit corresponding to location occupied by given category of object; Semantic = difference from word onset in cosine similarity calculated between current semantic layer activation and semantic representation of given item (i.e. target, unrelated distractor, visual competitor, semantic competitor, phonological competitor)].

3. Discussion

The response of the model at the end of training demonstrated that the model was able to replicate low-literacy behaviour for phonologically-related and semantically-related distractors, even when including also a visual distractor. The model's predictions, at all stages of development, indeed, suggested that coarse-coding resulted in a growing effect of semantic and visual representations influencing eye-gaze behaviour, and a slight but evident effect of phonological distractors, even in the presence of visual distractors and with coarse-coding of the phonology.

Thus, the model was able to reproduce previous computational investigations of adult behaviour with fine-coding of phonological representations[27], as well as reproducing key behavioural effects from the visual world paradigm[12]. Indeed, data from a visual world paradigm with phonological, visual, and semantic distractors indicates behaviour that is very similar to that of the model unfolding over time[12]. Such data shows an early deviation of eye fixations to the phonological distractor which then recede, and are later overwhelmed by a growing effect of the semantic and the visual distractors, with these remaining in influence until the end of the trial. As with our previous simulations[25], the model's temporal dynamics are extremely close to those of human behaviour.

So, what are the reasons for this nuanced time-course of the different representational modalities during word recognition? In the model, we can precisely define the constraints that result in the temporal patterns of behaviour. Initially, the phonological form of the word becomes active in the model's integrative layer, then this is aligned with information from the visual display resulting in early but weak fixations to phonologically related objects. At a later stage, information from activated semantic properties of the spoken word in the semantic layer flows back into the integrative layer causing eye movements to begin to move to the semantically related object. The visually-related distractor is also slower in activation because it requires the phonology to generate a code for the visual properties that are to be observed in the object array, and so this too is a later effect than the initial phonological relatedness. However, though the visual and the semantic effects are indirectly triggered by the phonological input, they are longer-lasting and more robust than the phonologically related distractor. This may be because as the phonological signal is produced, the model eventually receives perfect information that the phonologically related object is not a match to the actual phonological input. However, the indirect generation of semantic and visual information from phonology never provides an explicit signal that the mismatch is suboptimal, which may be the reason why negative information from the phonology exerts a smaller effect in suppressing looks to these other distractor modalities.

Regarding predictions of the model for testing with children and low-literacy populations, the model's results are consistent with previous studies of different phonological encoding affecting activation of phonological information. As in Smith et al.[25], we found that the size of the phonological effect was much reduced compared to semantic distractor effects, and also as compared to a model with fine-coding of phonology[27], where the auditory stream is parsed into individual phonemes, rather than, as in the current simulation, into a syllable, or word-level representation. In contrast to the fine-coding results, coarse-coding did not result in early activation of the semantic properties of the phonological competitor. Therefore, at early stages of processing, semantic information was not available to drive fixation of the phonologically related distractor, hence early phonological effects were much reduced.

Furthermore, the model's results suggest that visual information would be encoded in a similar manner in low-literacy populations as in high-literacy groups. For visual and semantic effects there was no qualitative difference between the model's performance and that of behavioural data with all distractor types present[12], even with coarse-coded input. Thus, the effect of literacy affects only the nature of the effect of phonological distractors, and not the contribution of both semantic and visual information in word recognition. Similarly, for the developmental data, the modeling here makes predictions that addition of a visual distractor will not affect the developmental profile of the phonological distractor effects that increase as the learner acquires more experience of the language. The visual distractor may reduce the apparent size of the effect of a phonologically-related distractor, but not its qualitative contribution to behaviour.

Thus, the model provides an illustration of the benefits of considering the confluence of a rich, multimodal environment converging on the cognitive system. The cognitive structure as implemented in the model, then, is merely an associative network, thus subtle behaviour is entirely a consequence of constraints from the representations themselves, and the requirements of tasks that directly or indirectly activate individual representations. The value of such a multimodal approach to modeling language means that observations of phenomena, such as phoneme awareness ability, can be grounded in processes that make sense of the role of such skills in the language processing system. Fine-coding of phonological input, as demonstrated in comparisons between previous simulations using such phoneme-level segmented representations[27] versus the coarse-coding of the current model, enhances the role of phonology in word recognition, both by increasing the size of the influence of phonology and by introducing its influence earlier in the process of recognising a spoken word.

The modeling here presents an enterprise that draws together multiple sources of information to simulate language processing in the presence of various, sometimes competing, sources of information regarding the meaning and referent of a spoken word. The behavioural effects of the model, in terms of the role of different modalities, and the time-course of their influence, are emergent properties of the multiple, co-occurring sources of information that surround the listener, both in measures of competent adult performance as well as affecting development of the language processing system. Such apparently complex behaviour is thus the result of a very simple system reacting to multiple, complex representations for words.

Acknowledgments

The second author was supported by the Economic and Social Research Council (UK) (grant number ES/L006936/1).

References

1. Adrián, J. A., Alegria, J., & Morais, J. (1995). Metaphonological abilities of Spanish illiterate adults. *International Journal of Psychology*, **30(3)**, 329–351.
2. Alcock, K. J., Ngorosho, D., Deus, C., & Jukes, M. C. H. (2010). We don't have language at our house: Disentangling the relationship between phonological awareness, schooling, and literacy. *British Journal of Educational Psychology*, **80(1)**, 55–76.
3. Allopenna, P. D., Magnuson, J. S., & Tanenhaus, M. K. (1998). Tracking the time course of spoken word recognition using eye movements: Evidence for continuous mapping models. *Journal of Memory and Language*, **38(4)**, 419–439.
4. Anthony, J. L., & Francis, D. J. (2005). Development of phonological awareness. *Current Directions in Psychological Science*, **14(5)**, 255–259.
5. Burnham, D. (2003). Language specific speech perception and the onset of reading. *Reading and Writing*, **16(6)**, 573–609.
6. Caravolas, M., Volin, J., & Hulme, C. (2005). Phoneme awareness is a key component of alphabetic literacy skills in consistent and inconsistent orthographies: Evidence from Czech and English children. *Journal of Experimental Child Psychology*, **92**, 107–139.

7. Chater, N., & Manning, C. D. (2006). Probabilistic models of language processing and acquisition. *Trends in Cognitive Sciences*, **10(7)**, 335–344.
8. Friederici, A. D. (2002). Towards a neural basis of auditory sentence processing. *Trends in Cognitive Sciences*, **6(2)**, 78–84.
9. Gaskell, M. G., & Marslen-Wilson, W. D. (1997). Integrating form and meaning: A distributed model of speech perception. *Language and Cognitive Processes*, **12(5–6)**, 613–656.
10. Harm, M. W., & Seidenberg, M. S. (1999). Phonology, reading acquisition, and dyslexia: insights from connectionist models. *Psychological Review*, **106(3)**, 491–528.
11. Huettig, F., & Altmann, G. T. (2005). Word meaning and the control of eye fixation: Semantic competitor effects and the visual world paradigm. *Cognition*, **96(1)**, B23–B32.
12. Huettig, F., & McQueen, J. M. (2007). The tug of war between phonological, semantic and shape information in language- mediated visual search. *Journal of Memory and Language*, **57(4)**, 460–482.
13. Huettig, F., Singh, N., & Mishra, R. K. (2011). Language-mediated visual orienting behavior in low and high literates. *Frontiers in Psychology*, **2**, 285.
14. Hulme, C., Bowyer-Crane, C., Carroll, J. M., Duff, F. J., & Snowling, M. J. (2012). The causal role of phoneme awareness and letter- sound knowledge in learning to read combining intervention studies with mediation analyses. *Psychological Science*, **23(6)**, 572–577.
15. Levelt, W. J. (1999). Models of word production. *Trends in Cognitive Sciences*, **3(6)**, 223–232.
16. Mani, N., & Huettig, F. (submitted). The changing dynamics of word-referent mapping across development. *Manuscript submitted for publication.*
17. McClelland, J. L., & Elman, J. L. (1986). The TRACE model of speech perception. *Cognitive Psychology*, **18(1)**, 1–86.
18. Monaghan, P. & Nazir, T. (2009). Modelling sensory integration and embodied cognition in a model of word recognition. In J. Mayor, N. Ruh, & K. Plunkett (Eds.), *Connectionist models of behaviour and cognition II*, pp.337–348. Singapore: World Scientific.
19. Morais, J., Content, A., Cary, L., Mehler, J., & Segui, J. (1989). Syllabic segmentation and literacy. *Language and Cognitive Processes*, **4(1)**, 57–67.
20. Norris, D., & McQueen, J. M. (2008). Shortlist B: A Bayesian model of continuous speech recognition. *Psychological Review*, **115(2)**, 357–395.

21. Plaut, D. C., McClelland, J. L., Seidenberg, M. S., & Patterson, K. E. (1996). Understanding normal and impaired word reading: Computational principles in quasi-regular domains. *Psychological Review*, **103**, 56–115.
22. Seidenberg, M. S., & McClelland, J. L. (1989). A distributed, developmental model of word recognition and naming. *Psychological Review*, **96(4)**, 523–568.
23. Serniclaes, W., Ventura, P., Morais, J., & Kolinsky, R. (2005). Categorical perception of speech sounds in illiterate adults. *Cognition*, **98(2)**, B35–B44.
24. Smith, A. C., Monaghan, P., & Huettig, F. (2013). An amodal shared resource model of language-mediated visual attention. *Frontiers in Psychology*, **4**.
25. Smith, A.C., Monaghan, P., & Huettig, F. (2014). Literacy effects on language and vision: Emergent effects from an amodal shared resource (ASR) computational model. *Cognitive Psychology*, **75**, 28–54.
26. Smith, A.C., Monaghan, P., & Huettig, F. (submitted). Constraints on multimodal integration during spoken word processing: Testing predictions of a parallel integration model of language mediated visual attention. *Manuscript submitted for publication.*
27. Smith, A. C., Monaghan, P., & Huettig, F. (submitted). The multimodal nature of spoken word processing in the visual world: Language acquisition in a multimodal parallel integration model. *Manuscript submitted for publication.*
28. Weber, A., & Scharenborg, O. (2012). Models of spoken-word recognition. Wiley Interdisciplinary Reviews: *Cognitive Science*, **3(3)**, 387–401.
29. Yee, E., & Sedivy, J. C. (2006). Eye movements to pictures reveal transient semantic activation during spoken word recognition. *Journal of Experimental Psychology: Learning, Memory, and Cognition*, **32(1)**, 1–14.
30. Ziegler, J. C., & Goswami, U. (2005). Reading acquisition, developmental dyslexia, and skilled reading across languages: a psycholinguistic grain size theory. *Psychological Bulletin*, **131(1)**, 3–29.

How to Design Emergent Models of Cognition for Application-Driven Artificial Agents

Serge Thill* and David Vernon†
Interaction Lab,
School of Informatics,
University of Skövde,
541 28 Skövde, Sweden
E-mail: **serge.thill@his.se*, *†david.vernon@his.se*

Emergent models of cognition are attractive for artificial cognitive agents because they overcome the brittleness of systems that are fully specified in axiomatic terms at design time, increasing, for example, the ability to deal with uncertainty and unforeseen events. When the agent is created to fulfil specific requirements defined by a given application, there is an apparent conflict between the emergent (*i.e.* self-defining) nature of the agent's behaviour and the pre-specified (*i.e.* axiomatically-defined) nature of the requirements.

Here, we develop a framework for the design of emergent models of cognition whose behaviour can be shaped to fulfil application requirements while retaining the desired characteristics of emergence. We achieve this by viewing the artificial agent as forming an eco-system with the environment in which it is deployed. Consequently, the objective function that determines the agent's behaviour is cast in terms that factor in interaction with the environment (while not being controlled by it) and therefore implicitly includes the application requirements.

This framework is particularly relevant to application driven research where artificial agents are designed to interact with humans in a certain manner. We illustrate this with the example of robot-enhanced therapy for children with autism spectrum disorder.

Keywords: Emergent models of cognition; Application-driven research; Robot-enhanced therapy.

1. Models in cognitive science and new challenges from embodied theories

Typically, models of cognition serve the study of cognition itself. McClelland put it rather succinctly when he argued[1] that we should think of models as "tools for exploring the implications of ideas" (p 12), even though they are necessarily simplifications of the real thing. Traditional cognitive science is replete with examples from many paradigms (whether symbolic, subsymbolic, Bayesian, or others) that have successfully done just that.

Models have been useful in the cognitive sciences because they tend to be *explanatory* models of cognitive mechanisms. With the advent of embodied theories of cognition (according to which human cognition cannot simply be entirely reduced to abstract, amodal symbol manipulation), however, new challenges have appeared. These theories often lead, for instance, to a need for "embodying" the model. This is typically done with an artificial agent, which can be simulated or real.

These approaches have significant hurdles to overcome if the aim is to provide an explanatory model of human cognition. Robotic models, for instance, are limited by the robotic hardware available, in particular the fact that these do not provide anything resembling a human body, even if the robots used are described as "humanoid" and "embodied". Models "embodied" in simulated environments, meanwhile, lose a significant degree of realism since simulators simply cannot approximate the complex physics of reality. Like robotic models, they raise the question of whether a (simulated) non-human body is an acceptable abstraction of a human body but extend the issue to the environment itself.

It has been argued repeatedly[2,3] that an advantage of robotic models of cognition is that they are forcibly integrated because every process from sensory perception to the mechanisms of the cognitive behaviours of interest needs to be modelled. This is rarely true, however, as readily illustrated by – for instance – the complexities of computer vision forcing modellers to take short cuts in obtaining visual inputs, for example by assuming a process which returns coordinates of objects of interest[4] or by using coloured, easily-discriminable objects[5]. The promised "complete" modelling, from sensory perception to higher-level cognition is thus not necessarily given and adds to the non-human embodiment used in simplified environments (even when real robots are used) to create a model embodied in something that is entirely different from a human experience. In particular, although sensorimotor aspects are thought to fundamentally shape higher cognition, they are often the first to be simplified.

Additionally, it is not a given (even though this is often assumed) that merely instantiating a model in a robotic body overcomes the limitations of traditional symbolic approaches to (strong) AI that such models typically intend to address (by virtue of taking an embodied, as opposed to amodal symbol-processing, view of human cognition). For instance, although they are often presented as overcoming the problems illustrated by the Chinese Room argument[6], they tend to ignore that Searle, in the original paper[7], already rejected the "robot reply" – collecting inputs from sensors and manipulating them to produce motor outputs – as a way of achieving an AI to which genuine understanding and mental states can be attributed (see 6 for a fuller discussion).

However, this is not to say that they have no explanatory power (or indeed no utility!) at all. For example, even strongly abstracted models of sensorimotor mechanisms can provide insights into minimal requirements for the cognitive process of interest[3]. While not necessarily creating an account of cognitive mechanisms *per se*, such strategies can nonetheless constrain the search space. Similarly, theoretical models can explore how *changes* in embodiment might affect cognitive processes that depend on it[8].

Overall, therefore, the realisation that human cognition is embodied to a degree that cannot be abstracted away makes "exploring the implications of ideas" with computational models much more challenging. At the same time, however, robots also create an entirely new *raison d'être* for cognitive models, which does not rely on explanatory insights about human cognition: application-driven models for human-machine interaction. The remainder of this paper is dedicated to the discussion of such an example.

2. Non-explanatory uses of models

Issues in explanatory power notwithstanding, technological advances in a number of areas dealing with human-machine interaction[9–11] give models of cognitive mechanisms an important reason of existence: to interact proficiently with humans, such machines need at least a rudimentary *Theory of Mind* (ToM); an internal model that can be used to estimate mental states of humans, in particular their intentions, expectations and predicted reactions to actions by the agent[10,12].

Additionally, to create machines with a given human ability necessitates a mechanistic model of this ability. Whether or not the model provides an adequate explanation of the mechanisms underlying the cognitive behaviour in a human is irrelevant here; it is sufficient that the postulated mechanisms can be exploited by the artificial agent. In contrast with McClelland's take on the utility of models, such models (although of human cognitive phenomena) do not need to possess any explanatory power; appropriate behaviour according to specification when instantiated in an artificial agent, no matter how biologically implausible the underlying mechanisms, is sufficient.

A particular human phenomenon of interest here is the *emergence* of appropriate cognitive behaviours. It is generally not possible to fully specify the behaviour that artificial cognitive agents ought to display since that would require complete knowledge of every situation they are likely to encounter. Emergent models therefore do not specify agent behaviour axiomatically at design time; rather the agent discovers appropriate behaviour[a] itself as a partial consequence of its interaction with the world in which it is embedded, brought about by the system's self-organizing system dynamics. Properly employed, this reduces the brittleness of its behaviour while increasing its ability to adapt to new situations or deal with events that the system designers had not foreseen.

3. Emergent models in purpose-built artificial agents

The prevalent current trend[b] in artificial cognitive systems research is to focus on the creation of artificial agents for specific purposes (often defined by given application scenarios). This is in contrast with previous, more explorative, research lines in which the agents are for instance used to illustrate principles of morphological computation[16] or embodiment.[17]

As an example, consider the use of (partially autonomous) cognitive humanoid robots in therapeutic interventions with children who have autism spectrum disorder (ASD)[18]: so-called robot-assisted therapy (RAT) and robot-enhanced therapy (RET). Although significant research problems (pertaining for instance to the controller of the robot[10]) remain, it is the end users (the therapists using these robots) who determine what the behaviour of the robot should be. These requirements drive research on, for instance, suitable robot control.

It is therefore interesting to reflect on the relevance of *emergent* models of cognition in a context in which the required behaviour is defined and driven by a specific application, and the primary mechanistic purpose of a model is to ensure these requirements are satisfied. After all, the application-driven specification of the cognitive behaviour of a robot (or other artificial agent) seems at first glance to be at odds with emergent behaviour that, by definition, is not fully defined a priori.

---

[a]This emergent behaviour derives from a process whereby the agent continually strives to make sense of its environment through its interaction with that environment. Consequently, the system's understanding of its world is inherently specific to the form of the system's embodiment and is dependent on the system's history of interactions, *i.e.*, its experiences. This process of making sense of its environmental interactions is one of the foundations of a branch of cognitive science called *enaction*[13,14] and is related to the concept of radical constructivism[15].

[b]This trend is evident, for example, in current EU Horizon2020 funding schemes, which place an increased importance on application-driven research; that is, research whose content is specified by the needs of an application.

We argue, using the example case of RET for illustration, that there is a useful place for emergent models in an application-driven world despite the apparent contradiction in that the behaviour of the system has to be both emergent and specified a priori.

In RET, most research and interventions are focused either on basic mechanisms, such as imitation, or various basic cognitive-behavioural skills, such as joint attention and turn taking, both of which are related to core symptoms (e.g. communication and social interaction), disabilities, and impairments (e.g., lack of social skills). Indeed, the severity of autism is correlated with impaired imitation skills, joint attention, and turn taking.[19] As such, children with autism fail to imitate and to have joint attention episodes from an early age; a salient diagnostic marker for the disorder.[20] Recently, researchers have found that for children with ASD, imitation and joint attention acquisition improves in settings in which technological tools are involved[21–26]. Taking into account that ASD patients tend to learn more from the interaction with technology rather than from the interaction with human beings, robots might have the potential to be used in ASD therapies as intermediaries between human models and ASD patients[27].

Although strongly scripted, successful therapy depends on the robot adapting to the child's behaviour and engaging in a behaviour of its own that fosters continued interaction. That is, the robot has to anticipate the child's behaviour and act effectively in the ensuing interaction to fulfil the application-driven requirement of promoting robot-child engagement in the face of uncertainty in interaction. It must therefore be able to successfully predict outcomes of actions (thereby managing or reducing uncertainty) while maintaining interaction with the child. This is the essence of cognition and herein lies the key reason for the use of emergent cognitive systems in application-driven scenarios. The fact that all required behaviours are pre-defined by the application might suggest a pre-defined axiomatic model of cognition. It is not possible, however, to specify the use-case scenarios to the extent such an approach would require because it is not possible to control or predict exactly how a child will interact with a robot at all times during the intervention. Emergent models, in contrast, allow behaviour to arise *without having to define it functionally in axiomatic terms.*

The catch is the following: An agent's emergent behaviour is not controlled directly but is modulated by an embedded (or intrinsic) value system[28], creating a challenge for the deployment of emergent systems in pre-defined applications. This value system provides the motives that determine the agent's actions and guide its development. In particular, it mediates the saliency of environmental stimuli, flagging the occurrence of important stimuli, and triggering the formation of goals[29]. The research problem is therefore to (a) identify a value system that satisfies the conditions of emergence and facilitates application-compatible agent-environment interaction, and (b) cast it in *quantitative* form so that it can be used to modulate the robot's emergent behaviour.

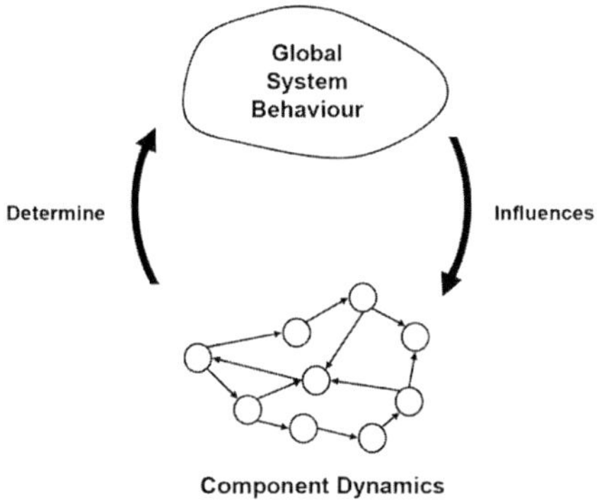

Fig. 1. Circular causality in cognition: global system behaviour influences the local components that determine the global behaviour in the first place (from [30]).

To address it, we make two propositions. First, artificial agents with emergent cognitive abilities should be considered as forming an eco-system with the environment in which they are deployed, much in line with situated views of human cognition. Consequently, the value system should be cast in terms of the predictive interaction with this environment. Second, the dynamics that govern the emergent self-organization of the system should be cast as a quantitative objective function that has the value system as one of its parameters. This objective function can be viewed as one or more policies that determine how each component in the system changes. It does not necessarily have to be fixed but can be adapted using, *e.g.*, reinforcement learning. The value system then shapes the objective function that governs the self-organization of the agent's constituent components which, in turn, give rise to the global system's behaviour.

This is effectively an instance of *circular causality*[31] (see Fig. 1): a cognitive agent's global behaviour is shaped by the dynamics of its local constituent components; simultaneously, these dynamics are influenced by the global behaviour[c]. To achieve desired behaviour by an artificial agent, we *shape and manipulate these local components.*

There are two key points to notice here. One is that the value system operates at the level of the global system, modulating the agent's behaviour and interaction with its environment. The other is that the objective function, parameterized in part by the state of the value system, operates at the level of the component dynamics and thereby governs the activity of the local components. Collectively, these component dynamics determine the global system behaviour in a circularly causal loop.

That the application constrains the emergent behaviour is then helpful since it requires the researcher to be very explicit about the desired interactions (again, without having to define them functionally), thus reducing the space in which the appropriate objective function can be found. Returning to the example of RET, a value system reflecting the need to maintain appropriate interactions with the child (allowing the system to increase its predictive capacity and tolerance to uncertainty) facilitates the emergence of interactive behaviours that also satisfy the application requirements, *i.e.* keeping the child engaged.

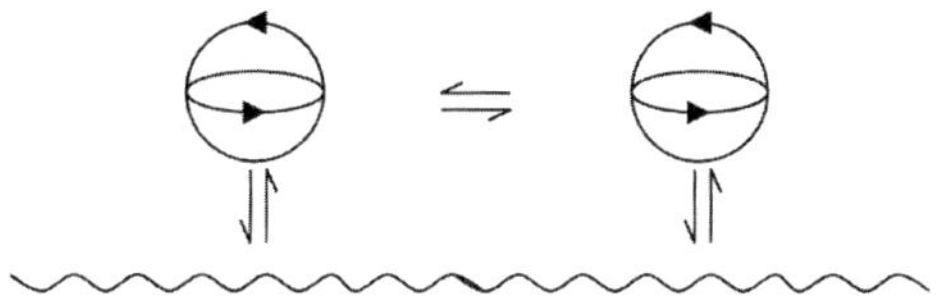

Fig. 2. Maturana and Varela's[34] ideogram depicting interaction between two agents, highlighting that interaction is a shared activity. (Picture from [30], where a detailed discussion can also be found).

The nature of interactive behaviour in emergent systems is captured well in Maturana's and Varela's ideograms[34] (for a more complete discussion, see 30) of self-organising and self-maintaining enactive systems. When two such agents exist, they are coupled in terms of the *shared activity* that is their interaction (see Fig. 2). When building an artificial agent, the desired behaviour is typically *specified in terms of this interaction.* Here, we therefore primarily consider artificial agents built to interact with humans for two reasons: (1) artificial agents are seldom created to exist in complete

[c]Closely related concepts include continuous reciprocal causation[32] and recursive self-maintanence[33].

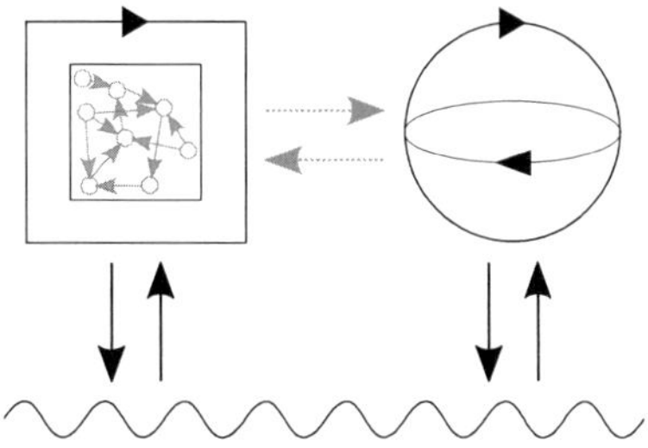

Fig. 3. Schematic of interaction between an artificial (left, square indicates that the agent is artificial) and another (right) agent that combines the concepts underlying Figs. 1 and 2. The appropriate behaviour emerges through appropriate configuration of the *local components* (in grey inside the artificial agent), yet the behavioural requirements are defined in terms of the *interaction between the agents* (in grey with dashed lines).

isolation from humans; interaction is often part of their purpose, and (2) interacting with another human intrinsically introduces uncertainty and events that cannot be anticipated in advance. As argued before, these conditions make the use of emergent models particularly relevant in the first place.

We have now prepared the scene for emergent models of cognitive behaviour: *the dynamics of the local components must lead to global behaviour that satisfies the requirements*[d] *defined by the desired interactions, and the emergent system's value system should be designed to favour these interactions, modulating the local dynamics to promote this global behaviour* (Fig 3). We now build on this characterisation to describe a framework for emergent models of cognition in application-driven scenarios.

4. How to design emergent models of cognition in purpose-built artificial agents

First, we note that we can describe the behaviour of the artificial agent in the terms of dynamical systems:

$$\dot{x} = \Phi\left(x, p, \eta\right) \tag{1}$$

Here, x denotes system state, p represents the system parameters, and η is a noise term[35]. The exact form of Φ is of course not known.

[d] A particular requirement could for instance be that this interaction be maintained; in other words, that it is undesirable for the artificial agent to either not produce any behaviour or to elicit no response from the interactant.

We can also describe the interaction between two agents X (artificial) and Y (human, say) from the perspective of the artificial agent:

$$P = F_n(x) \approx \tilde{y} \tag{2}$$

$$M = B_n(\tilde{y}) \approx x \tag{3}$$

F_n is a family of n forward models[e] that describes the predicted perception P of the agent X given some state x. It effectively says what the agent expects to see — of itself and of agent Y — if it executes some motor program corresponding to the state x. Here, y represents the actual behaviour intended by agent Y, while $\tilde{y}$ denotes the aspects of that behaviour perceivable by the artificial agent. In other words, this model allows the agent to *predict the outcome of its own actions and the actions of agent Y in terms of the possible action states.* It will, in practice, be learned using any appropriate choice amongst many existing approaches. This prediction can be compared to $\tilde{y}$, what it is actually perceiving, i.e., the behaviour of agent Y.

B_n, then, is a family of models similar to inverse models that define what action M the agent should carry out, given the observation $\tilde{y}$. This can be compared to what the agent X is currently doing, i.e. its state x. These models therefore allow the agent to *verify the appropriateness of its own actions* - if its actual actions do not match with what it should have been doing, then the actions are not appropriate. Consequently, Eqn. 3 is therefore given (and formulated[f]) by the application-driven requirements.

The designer of a system can specify the desired behaviour of the artificial agent through a suitable family of B_n models. In the case of RET, for example, B_n would encapsulate the requirements of the end-users (the therapists) and describe the desired ways in which the robot should interact with the child (for instance, through joint attention, imitation, and turn taking).

We can now define a value system that the artificial agent seeks to maximise. Effectively, a successful agent will have developed behaviour that ensures it can both accurately predict the outcome of its own actions

---

[e]Note that this characterization of a forward model differs slightly from the conventional notion. For example, the HAMMER architecture uses inverse models to identify the required motor commands required to achieve some internally-generated goal and forward models to predict the perceptual outcome of executing those commands.[36,37] In this case, however, the goal state is not a perception of the behaviour of agent X, but of the interactant agent Y.

[f]at least to some functional degree; possible refinements can still be learned later.

in terms of the interactant's behaviour *and* elicit appropriate behaviour from the interactant. Such a value system function Ψ can be formulated as follows.

$$\Psi\left(F_n\left(x\right), B_n\left(\tilde{y}\right)\right) \tag{4}$$

Given this value system function, we can now revisit the system behaviour as described by Eqn. 1. Specifically, replacing p with Ψ ensures that the behaviour of the system is now modulated by an objective function system based on the value system:

$$\dot{x} = \Phi\left(x, \Psi, \eta\right) \tag{5}$$

Since Ψ includes an evaluation of how well the agent's behaviour matches the task-specific requirements as specified by the B_n models, these requirements now shape what is otherwise emergent behaviour determined by the internal component dynamics of the artificial agent. This completes the core of what we have set out to do: Eqn. 5 effectively encapsulates a framework for the emergence of cognitive behaviour in an artificial agent that satisfies the requirements set by a given application. It also captures the essence of the circular causality described above, a key characteristic of emergent cognitive systems. The downward causality of the global system behaviour is captured by some function Ψ of (a) the agent's goal behaviour B as a function of its perceptions of the agent it is interacting with, and (b) its predicted perception of the behaviour of its interactant agent Y as a function of its possible behaviour x. The upward causality is the self-organizing function Φ which produces the component dynamics and hence the global behaviour, where this function has the downward value system state factored into it as a parameter.

Discovering a useful shape for Φ — necessary to ensure that the changes in the agent's behaviour bring it closer to the desired behaviour — is not trivial. We do however note that the problem might be usefully cast as a reinforcement learning problem[38]. The ability to maintain appropriate interactions with another agent in particular forms the basis of the reward signal which can guide modifications to Φ. Successfully maintaining such interactions, given a set of B_n models, would then also facilitate the emergence of interactive behaviours that satisfy the application requirements.

5. Discussion

There are (at least) three aspects worth considering to take this framework forward. The first is that Eqns. 2 and 3 are based on observable actions from both the artificial agent and the interactant. These actions are not instantaneous events but occur over some time – a fact that detailed implementations of the F_n and B_n models cannot ignore.

The second is that the framework at present purposefully ignores any implementation of a theory of mind (ToM) for the artificial agent.[10,12] This is because we wanted to highlight that the framework can be specified based solely on observable interactions and an approximation $\tilde{y}$ of what the underlying states of the interactant are (Eqn. 2). ToM models can be used to *predict* the states y, which in turn may be beneficial for the learning of a well-functioning family of forward models F_n.

The third concerns our replacing p with Ψ in Eqn. 1 – an act which requires more discussion in the context of autonomy. Emergent cognitive systems exhibit a considerable degree of autonomy. While there are many different types of autonomy[30], two are particularly relevent to the present discussion: behavioural and constitutive autonomy. Behavioural autonomy[g] focusses on the external characteristics of the system while constitutive autonomy focusses on the internal organization and the organizational processes that manage to keep the system viable and autonomous[41]. The constitutive-behavioural distinction is sometimes cast as a difference between *constitutive* processes and *interactive* processes[42,43]. Constitutive processes deal with the system itself, its organization, and its maintenance as a system through on-going processes of self-construction and self-repair. On the other hand, interactive processes deal with the interaction of the system with its environment. Both processes play complementary roles in autonomous operation of the system.

In this paper, we have focussed on the behavioural aspects of the agent, factoring in the value system into the objective function that governs the self-organization of the agent and hence its emergent behaviour. In doing so, we replaced p with Ψ in Eq. 1, and it can be argued that we were perhaps a little too quick to do so. The intrinsic value system Ψ modulates behaviour based on cognitive interaction with the environment; we might refer to it as a *behavioural value system*. However, there is different, *endogenous* value system that modulates the constitutive processes in the agent and is equally important to the autonomy of the agent and its emergent self-organization. This value system function would have been responsible for adaptively setting the parameter values p in Eq. 1. So, to complete the

[g]Behavioural autonomy is sometimes referred to as adaptive or cognitive autonomy to reflect its focus on interactive processes rather than constitutive processes[39,40].

picture, we must recognise that we need to include a second *constitutive* value system function, Ψ', to complement the *behavioural* value system function, Ψ, discussed above.

6. Conclusion

We have illustrated a symbiotic benefit between emergent systems and given application niches: the former are necessary to deal with the inherent uncertainty in deploying artificial systems to, for instance, interact with humans while the latter facilitate the clear specification of an objective function that in turn facilitates the emergence of desired behaviour.

The framework we have developed here capitalises on these insights to facilitate the use of emergent models of cognition in artificial agents created for specific applications. In the larger context of models of human cognition, it is an example that builds on properties of human cognition – emergence and autonomy – and has a clear use for ToM mechanisms. This highlights that the utility of models of human cognition goes beyond the exploration of the consequences of ideas (although this of course remains another important use of these models); they are also a necessity for the design of artificial agents that interact with humans.

Acknowledgements

This work has been supported by the EC FP7-ICT project DREAM (www.dream2020.eu), project number 611391.

References

1. J. L. McClelland, The place of modeling in cognitive science, *Topics in Cognitive Science* **1**, 11 (2009).
2. A. F. Morse, C. Herrera, R. Clowes, A. Montebelli and T. Ziemke, The role of robotic modelling in cognitive science, *New Ideas in Psychology* **29**, 312 (2011).
3. G. Pezzulo, L. W. Barsalou, A. Cangelosi, M. H. Fischer, K. McRae and M. J. Spivey, The mechanics of embodiment: a dialog on embodiment and computational modeling, *Frontiers in Psychology* **2** (2011).
4. J. Bonaiuto, E. Rosta and M. A. Arbib, Extending the mirror neuron system model, I, *Biological Cybernetics* **96**, 9 (2007).
5. A. F. Morse, T. Belpaeme, A. Cangelosi and L. B. Smith, Thinking with your body: Modelling spatial biases in categorization using a

real humanoid robot, in *Proceedings of the 32nd Annual Conference of the Cognitive Science Society*, eds. S. Ohlsson and R. Catrambone (Cognitive Science Society, Austin, TX, 2010).

6. T. Ziemke and S. Thill, Robots are not embodied! conceptions of embodiment and their implications for social human-robot interaction., in *Proceedings of Robo-Philosophy 2014: Sociable robots and the future of social relations*, (IOS Press BV, Amsterdam, NL, 2014).
7. J. R. Searle, Minds, brains, and programs, *Behavioral and Brain Sciences* **3**, 417 (9 1980).
8. S. Thill, H. Svensson and T. Ziemke, Modeling the development of goal-specificity in mirror neurons, *Cognitive Computation* **3**, 525 (2011).
9. B. Scassellati, How social robots will help us to diagnose, treat, and understand autism', *Robotics research* **552-563** (2007).
10. S. Thill, C. Pop, T. Belpaeme, T. Ziemke and B. Vanderborght, Robot-assisted therapy for autism spectrum disorders with (partially) autonomous control: Challenges and outlook, *Paladyn* **3**, 209 (2012).
11. S. Thill, P. E. Hemeren and M. Nilsson, The apparent intelligence of a system as a factor in situation awareness., in *Proceedings of the 4th IEEE International Multi-Disciplinary Conference on Cognitive Methods in Situation Awareness and Decision Support*, (San Antonio, TX, 2014).
12. B. Scassellati, Theory of mind for a humanoid robot, *Autonomous Robots* **12**, 13 (2002).
13. F. Varela, E. Thompson and E. Rosch, *The Embodied Mind* (MIT Press, Cambridge, MA, 1991).
14. J. Stewart, O. Gapenne and E. A. Di Paolo, *Enaction: Toward a New Paradigm for Cognitive Science* (MIT Press, 2010).
15. E. v. Glaserfeld, *Radical Constructivism* (RouteledgeFalmer, London, 1995).
16. R. Pfeifer, J. Bongard and S. Grand, *How the body shapes the way we think: a new view of intelligence* (MIT Press, Cambridge, MA, 2007).
17. A. D. Wilson and S. Golonka, Embodied cognition is not what you think it is, *Frontiers in Psychology* **4** (2013).
18. B. Scassellati, H. Admoni and M. Matarić, Robots for use in autism research, *Annual Review of Biomedical Engineering* **14**, 275 (2012), PMID: 22577778.
19. S. J. Rogers, S. L. Hepburn, T. Stackhouse and E. Wehner, Imitation performance in toddlers with autism and those with other developmental disorders, *Journal of Child Psychology and Psychiatry* **44**, 763 (2003).

20. C. Lord, M. Rutter, S. Goode, J. Heemsbergen, H. Jordan, L. Mawhood and E. Schopler, Autism diagnostic observation schedule: a standardized observation of communicative and social behavior, *Journal of Autism and Developmental Disorders* **19**, 185 (1989).
21. B. Scassellati, H. Admoni and M. Mataric, Robots for use in autism research, *Annual Review of Biomedical Engineering* **14**, 275 (2012).
22. D. J. Ricks and M. B. Colton, Trends and considerations in robot-assisted autism therapy, in *Proc. 1979 Int. Jt. Conf. Artificial Intelligence IEEE International Conference on Robotics and Automation (ICRA)*, (Anchorage, AK, 2010).
23. B. Robins, F. Amirabdollahian, Z. Ji and K. Dautenhahn, Tactile interaction with a humanoid robot for children with autism: A case study analysis involving user requirements and results of an initial implementation, in *Proc. Paper presented at the IEEE International Workshop on Robot and Human Interactive Communication (ROMAN)*, (Viareggio, Italy, 2010).
24. H. Kozima, C. Nakagawa and Y. Yasuda, Interactive robots for communication-care: A case-study in autism therapy, in *Proc. IEEE International Workshop on Robot and Human Interactive Communication (ROMAN)*, (Nashville, TN, 2005).
25. B. Vanderborght, R. Simut, J. Saldien, C. Pop, A. S. Rusu, S. Pineta and D. O. David, Using the social robot probo as a social story telling agent for children with asd, *Interaction Studies* **13**, 348 (2012).
26. A. Tapus, A. Peca, A. Aly, C. P. andL. Jisa, S. Pintea and D. O. David, Children with autism social engagement in interaction with nao, an imitative robot — a series of single case experiments, *Interaction Studies* **13**, 315 (2012).
27. D. David, S. A. Matu and O. A. David, Robot-based psychotherapy: Concepts development, state of the art, and new directions, *International Journal of Cognitive Therapy* **7**, 192 (2014).
28. P. Oudeyer, F. Kaplan and V. Hafner, Intrinsic motivation systems for autonomous mental development, *IEEE Transactions on Evolutionary Computation* **11**, 265 (2007).
29. K. E. Merrick, A comparative study of value systems for self-motivated exploration and learning by robots, *IEEE Transactions on Autonomous Mental Development* **2**, 119 (June 2010).
30. D. Vernon, *Artificial Cognitive Systems: A primer* (MIT Press, Cambridge, MA, 2014).

31. J. S. Kelso, *Dynamic patterns: The self-organization of brain and behavior* (MIT Press, Cambridge, MA, 1997).
32. A. Clark, *Being there: Putting brain, body, and world together again* (MIT Press, Cambridge, MA, 1997).
33. M. H. Bickhard, Autonomy, function, and representation, *Communication and Cognition-Artificial Intelligence* **17**, 111 (2000).
34. H. R. Maturana and F. J. Varela, *The tree of knowledge: The biological roots of human understanding.* (New Science Library/Shambhala Publications, 1987).
35. G. Schöner and J. A. S. Kelso, Dynamic pattern generation in behavioural and neural systems, *Science* **239**, 1513 (1988).
36. Y. Demiris and B. Khadhouri, Hierarchical attentive multiple models for execution and recognition (HAMMER), *Robotics and Autonomous Systems* **54**, 361 (2006).
37. Y. Demiris, L. Aziz-Zahdeh and J. Bonaiuto, Information processing in the mirror neuron system in primates and machines, *Neuroinformatics* **12**, 63 (2014).
38. M. E. Harmon and S. S. Harmon, Reinforcement learning: a tutorial, *WL/AAFC, WPAFB Ohio* **45433** (1996).
39. X. Barandiaran, Behavioral adaptive autonomy. A milestone in the Alife route to AI?, in *Proceedings of the 9th International Conference on Artificial Life*, (MIT Press, Cambridge: MA, 2004).
40. T. Ziemke, On the role of emotion in biological and robotic autonomy, *BioSystems* **91**, 401 (2008).
41. T. Froese, N. Virgo and E. Izquierdo, Autonomy: a review and a reappraisal, in *Proceedings of the 9th European Conference on Artificial Life: Advances in Artificial Life*, ed. F. A. e Costa et al. (Springer, 2007).
42. A. Moreno, A. Etxeberria and J. Umerez, The autonomy of biological individuals and artificial models, *BioSystems* **91**, 309 (2008).
43. T. Froese and T. Ziemke, Enactive artificial intelligence: Investigating the systemic organization of life and mind, *Artificial Intelligence* **173**, 466 (2009).

Competition Affects Word Learning in a Developmental Robotic System*

K. E. Twomey
ESRC International Centre for Language and Communicative Development
Lancaster University, Lancaster, UK
E-mail: k.twomey@lancaster.ac.uk
www.lucid.ac.uk

A. F. Morse[†] and A. Cangelosi[‡]
Centre for Robotics and Neural Systems
University of Plymouth, Plymouth, UK
E-mail: †anthony.morse@plymouth.ac.uk, ‡angelo.cangelosi@plymouth.ac.uk

J. S. Horst
School of Psychology
University of Sussex, Brighton, UK
E-mail: jessica@sussex.ac.uk

It is well-established that toddlers can correctly select a novel referent from an ambiguous array in response to a novel label, or fast-map. There is also a growing consensus that robust word learning requires repeated label-object encounters. However, the effect of the context in which a novel object is encountered is less clear. Horst, Scott & Pollard[1] presented toddlers with arrays of objects and asked them to choose the single novel object using a novel label, and showed that the more competitor objects children saw, the harder it was for children to retain that label. Here, we present a developmental robotic replication of this study using a variant of the Epigenetic Robotic Architecture[2] implemented in the iCub humanoid robot[3]. We discuss children's word learning in terms of the real-time processes governing the iCub's performance in the word learning task.

Keywords: Developmental robotics; Neural networks; Word learning; Fast-mapping.

1. Computational Insights into Young Children's Word Learning

Toddlers perform impressively when confronted with the seemingly difficult task of choosing the referent of a new word in an ambiguous environment[4]. A rich empirical literature shows that children reliably map a novel label to the single

* This work is supported by EU FP7 project Poeticon++ (no. 288382)

novel referent in an array of otherwise known objects, a phenomenon known as *fast-mapping*[5]. Even very young children have been shown to fast map given appropriate support (e.g., Mackenzie, Graham, Curtin & Archer[6]). There is also a growing consensus that over and above this quick initial mapping, robust word learning requires repeated encounters with the label and the target object[7,8,9]. Although we have a sound understanding of *what* children do in response to novel objects and labels, *how* they do it is less well understood. The apparent ease with which even very young children can solve the disambiguation task has prompted the proposal of innate, top-down word learning strategies; for example, Markman and Hutchinson[10] argued that children's tendency to map new words to taxonomically- but not thematically-related items provided evidence of a *taxonomic bias*. Similarly, when confronted with an array of multiple familiar objects and a single unknown item, children preferentially map novel words to the novel referent, which has been taken as evidence for an a priori *mutual exclusivity bias* (e.g., Markman & Wachtel[11]). More recently, Golinkoff and colleagues[12] suggested that instead of hard-and-fast, core word learning biases, infants might acquire flexible constraints, or *lexical principles*, over learning. Infants equipped with such lexical principles could exhibit the robust fast mapping observed in empirical tasks, but could also override them in situations where other information (e.g., social cues) might be a more reliable indicator of the referent of a novel word. An alternative, *associative learning* account proposes that fast mapping and subsequent word learning operates from the bottom-up, with associations between words and referents being made and strengthened over time, without the need for high-level, metacognitive reasoning abilities (e.g., [13]).

Recently, computational work has begun to address the issue of which of these mechanisms best explains fast mapping and word learning. Computational methods allow us to explore the perceptual and cognitive processes underlying empirically observed behavior[8,14]. Computational models of word learning simulate how children behave (e.g., pointing to the flamingo and not the dog or the fish) based on what they see and hear (e.g., one novel object, two known competitor objects and the novel word *flamingo*). Just like children, many computational models have internal representations which change with learning. In sharp contrast to children, however, we can inspect these representations as they develop over time. Thus, by examining the mechanisms driving representational change in the model, we can build an explicit account of the mechanisms which drive cognitive development in the child[15].

2. Target Empirical Data: The Effect of Referent Competition on Word Learning

There has been a particular interest in the word learning literature in children's fast mapping in referent selection tasks, in which they know the name for all-but-one of the objects they see. Various accounts of this behaviour have been proposed (for review, see [16]). Horst, Scott and Pollard (2010; henceforth HSP)[1] designed an empirical task to test the predictions of two of these accounts: *mutual exclusivity*[11] (ME) and novel-name-nameless-category[12] (N3C) The ME account assumes that children map novel names to novel objects by first ruling out competitor objects. For example, if the black and white toy animal is a *cow*, and the red toy vehicle is a *bus*, then the word *blicket* must refer to the new, nameless toy. ME therefore predicts increasing the amount of competitor objects present during referent selection should affect children simply map novelty to novelty; that is, the word *blicket* maps to the new, nameless toy, because both are novel. On this account the number of competitors present should make no difference to disambiguation or to word learning.

HSP pitted these predictions against each other in a word learning task. Specifically, they presented 36 30-month-old children with referent selection trials consisting of an array of 3D age-appropriate toys, one of which was novel and the rest of which were known to children. Critically, HSP varied between conditions the number of competitor objects seen during referent selection: trials consisted of a novel object and two, three, or four known competitors. In the two competitor condition, for example, a trial might consist of a plastic cone with multicoloured strings attached to it, a small plastic horse, and a small plastic block. In the four competitor condition, a trial might consist of the cone, the horse, the block, a spoon and a toy car. All other aspect of the design were held constant.

During the referent selection phase, children were presented with four sets of objects, across eight referent selection trials. Each novel object was presented twice and served as a target once. On each trial, children were allowed to look at the objects for three seconds before being asked to select either a known or the novel object (e.g., *known trial*: "Can you show me the horse?"; *novel trial*: "Can you show me the *fode*?"; five times per target; thus, two trials per set.) Children therefore had an equal amount of experience with each novel target during referent selection.

After referent selection children were presented with four test trials. Each of the four novel targets appeared on each test trial, and children were asked for each object in turn. If children had retained the novel label-object mappings formed during the referent selection phase, then they should pick the target object at levels greater than expected by chance (25%).

In line with existing studies, children were very good at referent selection, performing significantly above chance on both known and novel trials regardless of the number of competitors present. However, only children in the two competitor condition retained novel labels at levels greater than expected by chance, and did so significantly more reliably than children in the three and four competitor conditions (see light blue bars, Fig. 2). An analysis of reaction times during referent selection revealed that children in the two competitor condition selected novel objects marginally faster than children in the four competitor condition. Importantly, when reaction times were weighted by the number of competitors present, they did not differ between conditions. Thus, reaction times were related to the number of objects they saw, and children who retained label-object mappings after seeing the fewest objects were significantly faster to make those mappings than children who saw the most objects. The authors reasoned that the disambiguation task in the two competitor condition was less onerous in terms of processing capacity than in the other conditions. Put differently, these children only had to identify two known objects before mapping the novel label to the novel referent – a quicker and simpler undertaking than identifying three or four known objects.

The authors concluded that fast-mapping – and eventual word learning – involves paying attention to competitor objects in order to establish what the referent is *not*, as well as paying attention to the novel object, to establish what it is (see also Zosh, Brinster & Halberda[17] for evidence of the importance of competitor objects to the disambiguation task). On this account, fast-mapping is influenced not only by novelty, but also by knowing the names of the competitor objects; subsequent word learning is therefore the product of learning which associations are correct (e.g., novel object-*fode*), but also of learning which are wrong (e.g., cow-*fode*; see also McMurray et al.[8]) . The implication, therefore, is that word learning emerges from the interaction of multiple timescales of development: long-term experience (children's known vocabularies), medium-term cross-situational learning (multiples exposure to target/label mappings) and in-the-moment fast-mapping[8].

Importantly, however, HSP's children could have solved the referent selection task in more than one way. They could have used explicit, meta-cognitive reasoning; indeed, if children thought to themeselves "If I know that this black-and-white animal is called *cow*, and that this red vehicle is called *bus*, then that new thing must be called *blicket*" they would exhibit exactly the behaviour captured in HSP's task. However, associationist accounts of word learning claim that such apparently complex reasoning can emerge from the formation and strengthening over time of simple mappings between labels and referents, without the need for any top-down reasoning ability[9]. In the next section we describe a test of this ability using an associative neural network implemented in an embodied robotic system.

3. The iCub and the Epigenetic Robotics Architecture

In summary, HSP's children did not learn novel label-object mappings when exposed to the target object in the context of more than two competitor objects during the referent selection phase. Here, we explore the processes underlying these results using a version of the Epigenetic Robotics Architecture[2] (ERA) implemented in the iCub humanoid robot[3].

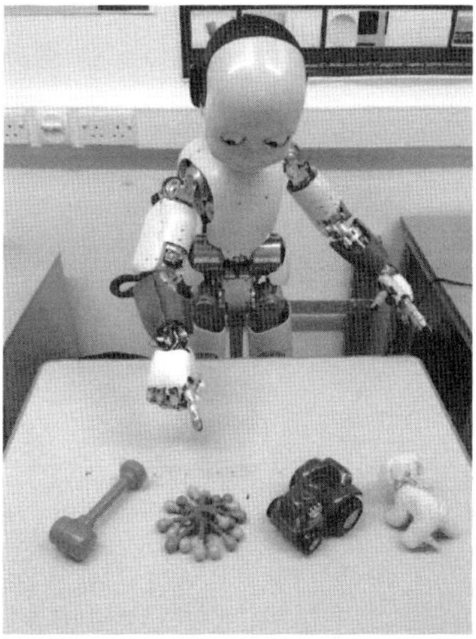

Fig. 1. iCub during referent selection

iCub's design reflects the physical proportions of a three-year-old child, with 53 degrees of freedom, and sensors, which encode a range of naturalistic perceptual input, approximating young children's perceptual environments (Fig 1). Thus, like children, iCub integrates visual, auditory, tactile and proprioceptive information to generate behaviour, for example auditory and visual information in a word learning task (although which modalities contribute to a given simulation are decided *a priori* by the modeller). Thus far, iCub has captured a diverse range of language acquisition data (e.g., affordance-based verb learning[18];

spatially-grounded noun learning[19]; the effect of category structure on word learning[14]; affordance-based adjective learning[20]).

The architecture employed in the current project was based on the ERA previously used in a replication of a category label learning experiment[14]. The ERA consists of a network of Self-Organising Maps[21] (SOMs): connectionist networks that reorganise their internal structure based on a winner-takes-all response to input stimuli. At the end of learning, the SOM reflects the structure of the input in its own topological structure; that is, neurons that are close together in the network fire in response to perceptually similar stimuli (e.g., the colours red and pink). SOMs naturally lend themselves to categorisation of complex naturalistic stimuli such as the auditory and visual inputs generated by iCub's sensors.

The model comprises two visual SOMs which receive processed visual information from iCub's cameras. One map receives an HSV (a widely-used system for numerically encoding hue and saturation[22]) spectrogram of each object in view and so represents colour, and the other receives shape information about each object (circleness, squareness, convexity, elongation[23]). Speech recognition, via the commercial software Dragon Dictate™, was used to provide speech-to-text input for the words, where each word dynamically activates a single unit in a "label" field. The visual SOMs are bidirectionally coupled to the units in the label field via Hebbian-like links to form a dynamic spreading activation network. Objects which are activated cause iCub to look at them or to reach and point to them.

For an object in a particular region, colour information is extracted by determining the location in HSV colour space of each pixel in that region. Ignoring the white background of the table, pixels with a saturation value greater than a threshold of 0.2 are allocated to one of 36 bins each representing 10 degrees of the 360 degree HSV hue continuum, which generates a histogram-like colour profile for each object. Each object profile is unique and based on the entire range of the colour SOM, allowing the model takes into account differences between uniformly and multicoloured objects.

Input SOMs were initialised with random connection weights. The 20 objects used in this study were simultaneously placed in view and the SOMs trained using standard equations 1 (SOM activity) & 2 (SOM learning rule):

$$BMU = Max_i\left(1 - \sqrt{\sum(a_j - w_{ij})}\right) \tag{1}$$

$$\Delta w_{ij} = \alpha exp\left(-\frac{dist^2}{2size}\right)(a_j w_{ij}) \tag{2}$$

The Best Matching Unit (*BMU*) is the unit with weights (w) most closely matching the current input vector (a). The weights of each node within the neighbourhood of the BMU are then modified to move closer to the current input vector, scaled according to the distance of this node from the BMU in the space of the SOM (i.e., not in terms of the input space).

The neighbourhood size and learning rate both monotonically decrease until the neighbourhood size is 1, at which point both the neighbourhood size and the learning rate of the SOM are fixed to allow learning to continue at a low rate.

The two SOMs and the label field are fully connected via Hebbian links subject to spreading activation and learning as in equations 3 (IAC Spreading Activation) & 4 (Hebb-like learning rule):

$$net_i = \sum w_{ij}a_j + \beta BMU_i \tag{3}$$

If $net_i > 0$

$$\Delta a_i = (\max - a_i)net_i - decay(a_i - rest)$$

Else

$$\Delta a_i = (a_i - min)net_i - decay(a_i - rest)$$

The net input to each unit in the whole network is the sum of spreading activation plus external activation if this node happens to be the BMU of a SOM or a currently active word. The experiment reported here used the parameter values: External Input Bias = 0.5; Max = 1; Min = -0.2; Decay = 0.5; Rest = -0.01.

If a_i OR $a_j > 0$: (4)

if $a_i\,a_j > 0$

$$\Delta w_{ij} = \lambda a_i a_j (1 - w_{ij})$$

else

$$\Delta w_{ij} = \lambda a_i a_j (1 + w_{ij})$$

The Hebb-like learning rule increases the strength of a connection if both units connected by this weight are positively active or reduces the strength of the weight if only one is positively active, and scales that change according to the product of their activity and how close the weights are to 1 or -1 respectively for positive and negative weight changes. Finally each field or pool is fully connected by fixed inhibitory connections. The experiment reported here used the parameter value $\lambda = 0.005$.

Note that adaptive connections exist only between the SOMs and label field, while constant-valued (-0.8) inhibitory spreading activation connections exist within each SOM and within the label field.

4. Simulating Word Learning in a Robotic System

4.1. *Procedure*

The procedure in the robot experiment was kept as close as possible to the procedure in the empirical task. As in the empirical study, the experiment was run 12 times per condition and trial order and counterbalancing were the same. In addition, we simulated the three developmental timescales that McMurray et al.[8] argue allow word learning to emerge via fast-mapping.

4.1.1. *Long-term vocabulary learning*

To simulate children's vocabularies, we taught the robot a vocabulary of "known" labels in an initial training session during which the robot was not exposed to the novel words used in the subsequent experiment. The SOMs were provided with object and label input for the 18 competitor objects it would encounter during the referent selection phase. For each individual object, the experimenter placed the object centrally in the robot's field of vision on a white surface and allowed the SOMs to settle – equivalent to allowing the children to look at the objects before providing the target label. Once the SOMs had settled (that is, once the system had formed a representation of that object), the experimenter provided the label SOM with the appropriate input, keeping the object in view (equivalent to the ostensive labelling shown to facilitate word learning in children[24]). Each object received 20 unambiguous labelling events. Thus, the robot began the experiment with a robust known vocabulary.

4.1.2. *In-the-moment referent selection*

The robot was presented with the same referent selection and test trials as children in the empirical task, again across two, three and four competitor conditions. During referent selection the robot was presented with four sets of objects on a white tabletop via eight fast-mapping trials. Each set consisted of a novel object and two, three or four known competitors selected from the pre-trained set (see Fig. 1 for an example referent selection trial). As in HSP, object locations and trial order were pseudorandomised across trials. Thus, the same set of objects was never presented on successive trials, known/novel trials occurred no more than twice in succession and each novel label/object pair was encountered in first, second, third or last position equally often. All objects were placed in the robot's field of vision and the SOMs were allowed to settle (equivalent to the three-second pause before labelling in the empirical study). Then, the experimenter labelled the object five times with either a known (pretrained) or novel label. Following labelling, the robot moved its head to centre its field of vision on each object in turn. This caused a node in the label SOM to become activated. If the SOM activated the appropriate label node for the target object, the robot's response was scored as correct, and if not, the robot's response was scored as incorrect. For example, on a known trial, activation of the *horse* node in response to the horse stimulus would be scored correct, and activation of the *yok* label would be scored as incorrect. Each novel object was presented twice and served as a target once. Object locations and trial order were pseudorandomised as in the empirical study.

4.1.3. *Word learning*

After referent selection the robot was presented with four test trials that proceeded in an identical manner to the referent selection trials. As in the empirical study, each of the four novel targets appeared on each test trial, and each served as the target on one trial. If the model had learned and retained novel label-object mappings during the referent selection phase, then it should activate the appropriate label node in response to each novel object at levels greater than expected by chance.

4.2. *Results*

Results from the robot task are depicted in Figure 2. In line with a previous simulation of a related fast-mapping task[14,25], the model successfully mapped known names to known objects and novel names to novel objects during referent selection, and did so at levels greater than expected by chance (100% correct on all known trials, all $ps < .0001$ on novel trials; all ps two-tailed; note that chance = 0.33, 0.25 and 0.20 in the two, three and four competitor conditions, respectively). Thus, the model captured HSP's referent selection results. At test, the model retained novel label-object mappings at levels greater than expected by chance (0.25) in the two competitor condition only (two competitor: $t(11) = 8.86$, $p < .0001$, $d = 5.34$; three competitor, $t(11) = 1.39$, *ns.*, $d = 0.84$; four competitor, $t(11) = 0.56$, *ns.*, $d = 0.34$). We submitted the model's proportion of correct choices on test trials to an ANOVA with condition as a between-subjects factor. This revealed a significant effect of Condition, $F(1,34) = 34.19$, $p < .0001$, $\eta_p^2 = 0.50$. Planned comparisons revealed that the model made significantly more correct choices in the two competitor condition than in the three or four competitor conditions (both $ps < .0001$). Thus, the model's responding at test also captured that of the children.

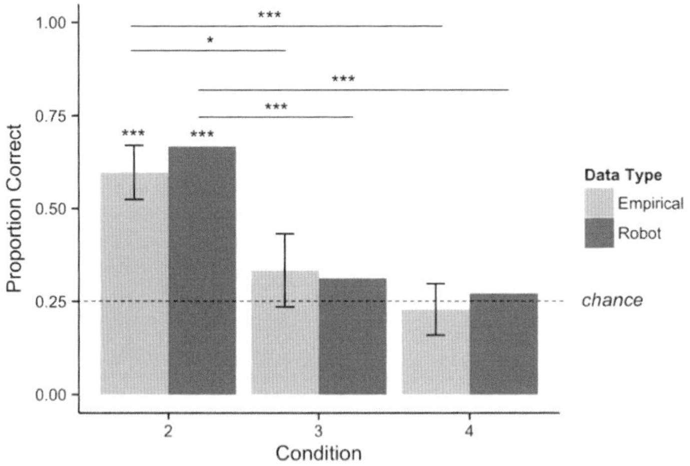

Fig. 2. Proportion correct of children's (light grey bars) and the model's correct choices (dark grey bars) at test. *** $p < .001$, ** $p < .01$, * $p < .05$.

5. Discussion

In the current study we used an embodied neural network model[2,3] to replicate 30-month-old children's behaviour in a word learning task[1]. Children in the empirical task were presented with a referent selection phase in which they were asked to select novel objects in response to novel names, from an array in which all other objects were known. When tested on retention of novel label-object mappings, only children who had initially encountered novel objects alongside two competitors successfully retained those mappings; children who saw more competitors did not retain novel labels. We taught the model a known vocabulary and then presented it with a maximally similar task. The model correctly mapped known and novel names to the appropriate objects during referent selection – that is, the model exhibited the same in-the-moment fast-mapping as the children. At test, only when novel objects had initially been encountered alongside two (but not three or four) competitors did the model successfully retain label-object mappings. Again, then, the model exhibited the same word learning behaviour as the children.

This simulation supports HSP's account of the processes underlying children's fast-mapping and word learning, and demonstrates that fast-mapping involves attention to known competitor objects as well as encoding the novel object-label mapping. Specifically, fast-mapping in the model occurs because inhibition from the strong known label-known object connections prevents the formation of new known label-novel object connections. Thus, during referent selection the only readily-available mapping is between the novel label and the novel object (see also [8]; [14]).

Importantly for the current study, however, time is key to capturing children's behaviour at test. Specifically, during referent selection the robot is provided with a label, which causes a spike of activation in the relevant label node. The robot then "looks" at each object in turn to establish whether the current label is associated with each object. After looking at all objects in the array, learning is applied. However, the activation in the label node decays over time. Thus, after the robot has encoded five objects (i.e., one target and four competitors), activation in the label node is lower than after the robot has encoded three objects (i.e., one target and two competitors). Thus, the novel label-object mappings formed in the three and four competitor conditions are weaker than the equivalent mappings formed in the two competitor condition; so weak, in fact, that the model is unable to use them to choose the correct object at test. Thus, consistent with McMurray et al.[8], we provide an explicit, mechanistic account of this word learning behaviour as emergent from the interaction between long-term learning (its pretrained, "known" vocabulary), its cross-situational learning, and its in-the-moment fast-mapping. However, the current study adds to this account the effect of micro-level temporal dynamics as instilled by activation decay during the time taken to look from one object to another. HSP note that children spent approximately 0.5s observing each object, irrespective of condition. Taken together, these studies demonstrate that word learning is an exquisitely sensitive and flexible process.

The current study is one of the first full-scale replications of a fast-mapping experiment using an embodied robotic system, and is the first to examine the effect of context on word learning via fast-mapping. As such, it contributes in a broader sense to the emerging interdisciplinary literature in the cognitive sciences that in recent years has begun to apply mathematical and computational innovations to some of the decades-old puzzles of developmental psychology[8,26,27], while helping us build an explicit account of the complex and subtle temporal, environmental and physiological interactions that govern word learning and cognitive development.

References

1. Horst, J. S., Scott, E. J., & Pollard, J. P. (2010). The role of competition in word learning via referent selection. *Developmental Science*, **13(5)**, 706–713.
2. Morse, A. F., de Greeff, J., Belpeame, T., & Cangelosi, A. (2010). Epigenetic Robotics Architecture (ERA). *Autonomous Mental Development, IEEE Transactions on Autonomous Mental Development*, **2(4)**, 325–339.
3. Metta, G., Natale, L., Nori, F., Sandini, G., Vernon, D., Fadiga, L., & Montesano, L. (2010). The iCub humanoid robot: An open-systems platform for research in cognitive development. *Neural Networks*, **23(8-9)**, 1125–1134.
4. Quine, W. V. O. (1960). *Word and object: An inquiry into the linguistic mechanisms of objective reference*. Cambridge: MIT Press.
5. Carey, S., & Bartlett, E. (1978). Acquiring a single new word. *Papers and Reports on Child Language Development*, **15**, 17–29. doi:10.1037/0012-1649.38.6.967
6. MacKenzie, H. K., Graham, S. A., Curtin, S., & Archer, S. L. (2014). The flexibility of 12-month-olds' preferences for phonologically appropriate object labels. *Developmental Psychology*, **50(2)**, 422–430. http://doi.org/10.1037/a0033524
7. Horst, J. S., & Samuelson, L. K. (2008). Fast mapping but poor retention by 24-month-old infants. *Infancy*, **13(2)**, 128–157. doi:10.1080/15250000701795598
8. McMurray, B., Horst, J. S., & Samuelson, L. K. (2012). Word learning emerges from the interaction of online referent selection and slow associative learning. *Psychological Review*, **119(4)**, 83877. doi: 10.1037/a0029872
9. Smith, L., & Yu, C. (2008). Infants rapidly learn word-referent mappings via cross-situational statistics. *Cognition*, **106(3)**, 1558–1568.
10. Markman, E. M., & Hutchinson, J. E. (1984). Children's sensitivity to constraints on word meaning: Taxonomic versus thematic relations. *Cognitive Psychology*, **16(1)**, 1–27.
11. Markman, E. M., & Wachtel, G. F. (1988). Children's use of mutual exclusivity to constrain the meaning of words. *Cognitive Psychology*, **20(2)**, 121–157.

12. Golinkoff, R. M., Hirsh-Pasek, K., Bailey, L. M., & Wenger, N. R. (1992). Young-Children and Adults Use Lexical Principles to Learn New Nouns. *Developmental Psychology*, **28(1)**, 99–108.
13. Smith, L. B. (2000). Learning how to learn words: An associative crane. In R. M. Golinkoff, K. Hirsh-Pasek, L. Bloom, L. B. Smith, A. L. Woodward, N. Akhtar, M. Tomasello & G. Hollich (Eds.), *Becoming a Word Learner: A Debate on Lexical Acquisition* (pp. 51–80). New York: Oxford University Press.
14. Twomey, K. E., Horst, J. S., & Morse, A. F. (2013). An embodied model of young children's categorization and word learning. In L. J. Gogate & G. Hollich (Eds.), *Theoretical and Computational Models of Word Learning: Trends in Psychology and Artificial Intelligence* (pp. 172–196). Hershey, PA: Information Science Reference.
15. Westermann, G., & Mareschal, D. (2012). Mechanisms of developmental change in infant categorization. *Cognitive Development,* **27(4)**, 367–382.
16. Halberda, J. (2006). Is this a dax which I see before me? Use of the logical argument disjunctive syllogism supports word-learning in children and adults. *Cogn. Psychol.*, **53(4)**, 310–44. doi:10.1016/j.cogpsych.2006.04.003
17. Zosh, J. M., Brinster, M., & Halberda, J. (2013). Optimal contrast: Competition between two referents improves word learning. *Applied Developmental Science*, **17(1)**, 20–28. doi:10.1080/10888691.2013.748420
18. Marocco, D., Cangelosi, A., Fischer, K., & Belpaeme, T. (2010). Grounding action words in the sensorimotor interaction with the world: experiments with a simulated iCub humanoid robot. *Frontiers in Neurorobotics*, **4**.
19. Morse, A. F., Belpaeme, T., Cangelosi, A., & Smith, L. B. (2010). Thinking with your body: Modelling spatial biases in categorization using a real humanoid robot. In S. Ohlsson & R. Catrambone (Eds.), *32nd Annual Conference of the Cognitive Science Society*. Austin, TX: Cognitive Science Society.
20. Yürüten, O., Uyanık, K., Çalışkan, Y., Bozcuoğlu, A., Şahin, E., & Kalkan, S. (2012). Learning adjectives and nouns from affordances on the iCub humanoid robot. In T. Ziemke, C. Balkenius, & J. Hallam (Eds.), *From Animals to Animats 12* (Vol. 7426, pp. 330–340). Berlin: Springer.
21. Kohonen, T. (1998). The self-organizing map. *Neurocomputing*, **21(1-3)**, 1–6.
22. Alvy Ray, S. (1978). Color gamut transform pairs. *SIGGRAPH Computer Graphics*, **12(3)**, 12–19. doi:10.1145/965139.807361

23. Montesano, L., Lopes, M., Bernardino, A., & Santos-Victor, J. (2008). Learning object affordances: from sensory–motor coordination to imitation. *IEEE Transactions on Robotics*, **24(1)**, 15–26.
24. Axelsson, E. L., Churchley, K., & Horst, J. S. (2012). The right thing at the right time: why ostensive naming facilitates word learning. *Frontiers in Psychology*, **3**.
25. Twomey, K. E., Ranson, S. L., & Horst, J. S. (2014). That's more like it: Multiple exemplars facilitate word learning. *Infant and Child Development*, **23(2)**, 105–122.
26. Schlesinger, M. (2009). The robot as a new frontier for connectionism and dynamic systems theory. In J. P. Spencer, M. Thomas, & J. L. McClelland (Eds.), *Toward a Unified Theory of Development: Connectionism and Dynamic System Theory Re-Considered* (pp. 182–201). New York, NY: Oxford University Press.
27. Westermann, G., & Mareschal, D. (2014). From perceptual to language-mediated categorization. *Philosophical Transactions of the Royal Society B: Biological Sciences*, **369(1634)**, 20120391.
28. Markman, E. M. (1990). Constraints children place on word meanings. *Cognitive Science*, **14(1)**, 57–77.